OXFORD TEXTUAL PERSPECTIVES

The Globe in Print

GENERAL EDITORS

Elaine Treharne   Greg Walker

The Globe in Print

The Book of the Play in the Age of Shakespeare

STEPHEN ORGEL

OXFORD
UNIVERSITY PRESS

Great Clarendon Street, Oxford, OX2 6DP,
United Kingdom

Oxford University Press is a department of the University of Oxford.
It furthers the University's objective of excellence in research, scholarship,
and education by publishing worldwide. Oxford is a registered trade mark of
Oxford University Press in the UK and in certain other countries

© Stephen Orgel 2024

The moral rights of the author have been asserted

All rights reserved. No part of this publication may be reproduced, stored in
a retrieval system, or transmitted, in any form or by any means, without the
prior permission in writing of Oxford University Press, or as expressly permitted
by law, by licence or under terms agreed with the appropriate reprographics
rights organization. Enquiries concerning reproduction outside the scope of the
above should be sent to the Rights Department, Oxford University Press, at the
address above

You must not circulate this work in any other form
and you must impose this same condition on any acquirer

Published in the United States of America by Oxford University Press
198 Madison Avenue, New York, NY 10016, United States of America

British Library Cataloguing in Publication Data
Data available

Library of Congress Control Number: 2024932969

ISBN 9780198920557
ISBN 9780198920540 (pbk.)

DOI: 10.1093/oso/9780198920557.001.0001

Printed and bound by
CPI Group (UK) Ltd, Croydon, CR0 4YY

Links to third party websites are provided by Oxford in good faith and
for information only. Oxford disclaims any responsibility for the materials
contained in any third party website referenced in this work.

For
Deanne Williams and Tom Bishop

SERIES EDITORS' PREFACE

Oxford Textual Perspectives is a series of informative and provocative studies focused upon texts (conceived of in the broadest sense of that term) and the technologies, cultures, and communities that produce, inform, and receive them. It provides fresh interpretations of fundamental works, images, and artefacts, and of the vital and challenging issues emerging in English literary studies. By engaging with the contexts and materiality of the text, its production, transmission, and reception history, and by frequently testing and exploring the boundaries of the notions of text and meaning themselves, the volumes in the series question conventional frameworks and provide innovative interpretations of both canonical and less well-known works. These books will offer new perspectives, and challenge familiar ones, both on and through texts and textual communities. While they focus on specific authors, periods, and issues, they nonetheless scan wider horizons, addressing themes and provoking questions that have a more general application to literary studies and cultural history as a whole. Each is designed to be as accessible to the non-specialist reader as it is fresh and rewarding for the specialist, combining an informative orientation in a landscape with detailed analysis of the territory and suggestions for further travel.

Elaine Treharne and Greg Walker

PREFACE

I have been thinking about the publication of early modern plays for many years, and have written about the subject in a number of articles. The present volume is based on that work (the essays are cited in the notes), and on several courses I designed and taught during my thirty-two years at Stanford. In an excellent collection entitled *The Book of the Play* a couple of potshots are taken at S. Orgel for asserting that plays are not reducible to their texts, that the book of the play is not the play.[1] But the contributors' own arguments persuade me to stand my ground: essay after essay is devoted to showing how much revision was required to transform the play into a book. Claire Bourne, in a valuable work about the development of typography for printed drama, attempts a refutation of S. Orgel with a single example:

> When the publisher Richard Hawkins brought to press a third edition of Beaumont and Fletcher's *A King and No King*, he signaled this conflation of performance and print with a canny riddle on the title page:
>
> The Stationer to Dramatophilus
>
> > *A Play and no Play, who this Booke shall read,*
> > *Will iudge, and weepe, as if 'twere done indeed.*[2]
>
> Hawkins's marketing pitch was simple: the "*Booke*" could produce the same affective response as seeing "it" (the play, or its action) "*done indeed.*" By interpolating the reader as a lover of plays ("Dramatophilus"), Hawkins granted him expertise as a *play*-reader that would surely inform the decision to buy the quarto or not. Seeing it "*done indeed*" could refer to witnessing events dramatized in the play come to pass in real life. However, watching those same events performed by actors could also count as seeing them done *in deed*.

---

[1] Marta Straznicky, ed., *The Book of the Play* (Amherst: University of Massachussets Press, 2006), pp. 4, 52.

[2] Francis Beaumont and John Fletcher, *A King, and No King* (London: Richard Hawkins, 1631), sig. A2ı.

Hawkins's tiny epistle essentially promised that the book could—and would—trigger both an intellectual response ("judgment") and emotional one ("weeping"). In promising this, the publisher established a correspondence between the ways in which both stage and page effected plays and affected those who consumed them. Hawkins's couplet is a shrewd defense—even advocacy—of the book as a medium fit for the "peremptorie performance" or "second publication" of dramatic material. Furthermore, the paradox it presents preemptively solves the either/or dilemma evident in Stephen Orgel's well-known declaration: "If the play is a book, it's not a play." *A King and No King* (1631) was both play *and* book; and it was, in fact, its very bookishness that allowed it and every other play printed in early modern England to be recognized by their earliest readers *as plays* in the first place.[3]

But it all depends on how you interpret what you read. Bourne's example seems to me, on the contrary, to confirm my point: it is a marketing strategy that recognizes that books are not plays, and tries to spin the fact to the book's advantage. It is surely significant that this is Bourne's only example; the need for the publisher's denial is evidence of how widespread the counter-assumption was.

There are, in any case, a multitude of counter-examples, from all the transformations the scripts of plays had to go through to be transformed into books, to Ben Jonson rewriting his plays for publication and the publisher Humphrey Moseley asserting that the *real* play was the book, preserving "all that was acted and all that was not." Legal opinion in Shakespeare's time was quite clear on the subject. As I explain below, in 1610 a group of players in Yorkshire were arrested and charged with sedition. Their offense was performing *Pericles*, *King Lear*, and a lost play about Saint George that the authorities claimed were (or perhaps had had introduced into them) Roman Catholic propaganda—the members of the troupe were Catholic. In their defense the actors replied that their performing texts of *Pericles* and *King Lear* were the published quartos. Since these had been duly licensed for publication they could not be considered seditious. This was not, however, considered a sufficient defense: the court took the position that the licensing of books is a different matter from the licensing of play scripts. Plays are social events

---

[3] Claire Bourne, *Typographies of Performance in Early Modern England* (Oxford: Oxford University Press, 2020), p. 8.

involving crowds, and are therefore much more dangerous than individual readers or family groups. Books in 1610 were not plays. To argue that in modern usage a book may be a play is to acknowledge how much our sense of both drama and theater has changed. As D. F. McKenzie writes in a foundational text, "Meanings are not ... inherent but are constructed by successive interpretive acts by those who write, design and print books, and by those who buy and read them."[4]

In part this book is an expansion of my essay "Acting Scripts, Performing Texts."[5] That essay was addressed to specialists; this book assumes a readership with no prior knowledge of book history. Some of the work here also elaborates material in my book *The Idea of the Book and the Creation of Literature*.[6] I am indebted to Silvia Bigliazzi of the University of Verona, who commissioned what became Chapter 6; a version of it appears in *Memoria di Shakespeare* (Sapienza Università di Roma) 10.2023. Long ago Franco Giacobelli and more recently Alessandra Petrina, both of the University of Padua, kindly provided information about the annotated Shakespeare first folio at the University of Padua. Martin Butler declared himself as baffled as I am about Sir John Harington's account of the masque of Solomon and the Queen of Sheba, and Jason Scott-Warren, who knows more about Sir John Harington than anyone, kindly responded to a query about the mysterious Mr. Secretary Barlow, to whom Harington's account of the masque is addressed; Scott-Warren was similarly unable to identify him. I am grateful to Elaine Treharne and Greg Walker, the general editors of Oxford Textual Perspectives, for their enthusiasm for the project, to the anonymous press readers for helpful suggestions, and to my Oxford editor Hannah Doyle for her guidance. Michael Wyatt and Giorgio Alberti have been the best of listeners and the best of friends. Peter Stallybrass has been an intellectual beacon over the many years of our friendship. The dedication to Deanne Williams and Tom Bishop records a long friendship and a constant source of inspiration.

---

[4] D. F. McKenzie, *"What's Past Is Prologue,"* The Bibliographical Society Centennial Lecture, 1992 (London: Hearthstone Publications, 1993), p. 18.
[5] In my collection *The Authentic Shakespeare and Other Problems of the Early Modern Stage* (New York: Routledge, 2002), pp. 21–48.
[6] Oxford: Oxford University Press, 2023.

CONTENTS

List of Illustrations — *xv*
A Note on Quotations — *xvii*

1. The Drama of Print — 1
2. The Example of *Gorboduc* — 17
3. From Stage to Page — 39
4. The Example of *Macbeth* — 49
5. The Jonson Folios — 63
6. Classical Models — 81
   Conclusion — 101

Principal Works Discussed — 111
Bibliography — 113
Index — 121

LIST OF ILLUSTRATIONS

2.1. Thomas Middleton, *A Game at Chesse*, fol. 53^r Bridgewater manuscript, EL34 B17, The Huntington Library, San Marino, CA.   30

2.2. Thomas Middleton, *A Game at Chesse*, The Letter (3.1.33ff.), fols. 22^v–23^r, Bridgewater manuscript, EL34 B17, The Huntington Library, San Marino, CA.   31

2.3. The Letter, from two quartos of *A Game at Chesse*, STC (2nd edn) 17,882, fol. E4^r; and STC (2nd edn) 17,884, fol. E2^r.   33

3.1. Macbeth and Banquo meet the "Nimphes or Feiries." Raphaell Holinshed, *The Firste Volume of the Chronicles of England, Scotlande and Ireland* (1577), "The Historie of Scotlande," p. 243.   41

6.1. Henry Peacham, drawing based on *Titus Andronicus*, 1595–1614. Longleat, Portland Papers I F. 159v. Reproduced by kind permission of the Marquess of Bath, Longleat House.   90

6.2. G. P. Trapolin, the Chorus in *Antigone: tragedia* (Padova, 1581), p. 8. Folger Shakespeare Library, 169–641q.   93

6.3. *The seconde tragedie of Seneca entituled Thyestes faithfully Englished by Iasper Heywood* (London, 1560), fol. D8^r (detail). The Huntington Library, San Marino, CA, 51.961.   96

6.4. *Seneca His Tenne Tragedies, Translated into Englysh* (London, 1581), fol. 37^v (detail).   96

6.5. J[ohn] W[right], *Thyestes A Tragedy, Translated out of Seneca* (London, 1684), p. 87.   97

A NOTE ON QUOTATIONS

In quotations, u, v, i, j, and w have been normalized, and contractions have been expanded; otherwise, quotations are given as they appear in the editions cited. In the case of early books that do not include page numbers, citations are to signature numbers. Signatures are the marks placed by the printer at the beginning of each gathering (or quire) to show how the book is organized. The marks are usually letters or combinations of letters, but they may also be symbols, such as asterisks or pilcrows (paragraph signs). Thus fol. (for folio, or sig., for signature) $A2^r$ means the first side (*recto*) of the second leaf of the gathering marked A. The second side, or *verso*, would be $A2^v$. Shakespeare quotations are from the New Pelican editions, edited by myself and A. R. Braunmuller.

| 1 |

The Drama of Print

This is a book about the transformations the drama of the first great age of English theater underwent to become literature. What happens to a play when it becomes a book? The Globe of my title is not the world, but the most famous Elizabethan and Jacobean theater, the theater of Shakespeare, which claimed, in its name, to contain and represent the world—as Shakespeare's Jaques put it in *As You Like It*, "All the world's a stage." But asking how plays become books is not quite the same as asking how theater becomes literature—there are several steps in between, and the translation from stage to page is not merely a matter of transforming the dialogue of a spectacle into a reading text and then setting it in type. Behind the question is a much more basic question: Why do it? Theater has always been popular, but what is the audience for the book of the play? Who, beside the actors, would want to read the text of a play? Of course, readings are performances too, especially if they are readings aloud, as they generally were until relatively recently; and readers interpret the text through their own preconceptions, just as both performers and audiences do to the scripts that for them are the basis of the play. The play, moreover, has undergone various editorial interventions to transform it into a book, and, as anyone who has worked in theater knows, transforming the book back into a play is not a simple or straightforward process.

The earliest surviving reference to Shakespeare as a playwright is a hostile allusion in the cautionary romance *Greene's Groatsworth of*

Wit (1592), said to be the last work written by Robert Greene, but probably by somebody else whose identity is uncertain (the leading candidates are the writer and printer Henry Chettle and Greene's friend the satirist Thomas Nashe). Here is the passage: a well-educated gentleman reduced by poverty to writing plays warns other playwrights,

> there is an upstart Crow, beautified with our feathers, that with his *Tygers hart wrapt in a Players hyde*, supposes he is as able to bombast out a blanke verse as the best of you: and beeing an absolute *Johannes fac totum* [Jack of all trades], is in his owne conceit the onely Shake-scene in a countrey. (fol. F1v)

The "upstart crow" is Shakespeare, the country boy without a university education, who nevertheless thinks himself as good as highly educated playwrights like Robert Greene and Christopher Marlowe; "beautified with our feathers" has been taken to imply an additional charge of plagiarism, but probably only means that his plays imitate ours. The passage identifies Shakespeare as both playwright and performer (a "player" is an actor). "Tygers hart wrapt in a Players hyde" parodies the line "O tiger's heart wrapped in a woman's hide" from Shakespeare's early history play now known as *3 Henry VI* (1.4.137 in modern editions), preserved in the first folio as *The Third Part of Henry the Sixt with the death of the Duke of Yorke*, but known in its earliest published version as *The True Tragedie of Richard Duke of Yorke, and the death of good King Henrie the Sixt, with the Whole Contention betweene the two Houses Lancaster and Yorke*—there is no way of knowing what the play was called on the stage, before it became a book.[1] This alone is an indication of the transformations plays underwent when they became books, and how new editions involved further transformations. But what is especially striking is that the allusion was to a play not yet in print, which suggests a large theater audience with good memories who were also readers of satirical pamphlets.

We have printed and circulated the texts of plays to preserve them, enabling them to be performed, whether by actors or readers, widely and long after their creation. In an era of amateur theatricals that market

---

[1] In the earliest version of the play in print, where the title is *The True Tragedie of Richard Duke of Yorke*, etc. (1595) the line appears on fol. B2v.

would have been a substantial one. But there have always been solitary readers as well, for whom the book provided their only access to a drama they might have heard about but had no way of seeing; and there were also readers for whom drama, like any imaginative literature, was a source of wisdom and entertainment. Still, those various readerships had been well enough served by manuscript circulation, and it was many decades before printers had enough confidence in the market potential of drama to commit it to print.

Nevertheless, it has been shown that, contrary to a long and pervasive assumption, printing plays was good business:

> Judged by reprints, plays sold much better than the average book in Elizabethan and Jacobean England, much better even than sermons—a class of book that appears on [Peter] Blayney's best-seller list and that is widely considered one of the most popular in the early modern book trade. Plays were, in fact, among the most successful books in which an early modern stationer could choose to invest. They turned a profit more reliably than most other types of books, and this profit would not have been paltry, as many have claimed, but rather would have been fairly typical for an edition of books. Later, in Caroline England, the trade in printed plays was fundamentally transformed: plays were reprinted much less frequently, yet more editions were published than ever before. While we do not have space to examine in detail this "Caroline paradox"—in which plays seem to have become less popular by one standard and more popular by another—we will suggest that it points toward the development of a division in the playbook market between new plays and "classic" plays, a division that signals the emergence of an early modern canon of printed drama.[2]

Indeed, common sense would suggest that publishers would not have bothered with plays if they had not been profitable. Plays were typically

---

[2] Alan B. Farmer and Zachary Lesser, "The Popularity of Playbooks Revisited," *Shakespeare Quarterly*, 56.1 (Spring, 2005), 6, taking issue with Peter Blayney's essay, "The Publication of Playbooks," in *A New History of Early English Drama*, ed. John D. Cox and David Scott Kastan (New York: Columbia University Press, 1997), pp. 383–422. Blayney trades energetic rebuttals with Farmer and Lesser in *Shakespeare Quarterly*, Summer, 56.2 (Summer, 2005); both concede, not surprisingly, that it all depends on how you count and what you treat as evidence. Farmer and Lesser's conclusions are supported by Lukas Erne's Oxford Lyell Lectures (2012), published as *Shakespeare and the Book Trade* (Cambridge: Cambridge University Press, 2013).

published throughout the early modern era in small relatively inexpensive formats, quartos or octavos—the largest standard book size was the folio (the word means "leaf") for which the printing sheet consisted of two double-sided leaves, four pages, and the sheet was folded in half. Folios were large, expensive books, and were the format for serious and important works, typically philosophy, history, science, classics—publishing a collection of modern plays in folio constituted a considerable rise in dignity for popular drama. To produce a quarto (a "fourth") the printing sheet was folded again crosswise, producing four double-sided leaves, eight pages. For an octavo ("eighth") the sheet was folded again to make eight leaves and sixteen pages. Play quartos and octavos were typically sold unbound, merely stitched together with string, and most have not survived—Shakespeare quartos are now far rarer than Shakespeare folios, though they were produced in larger numbers. But to put the matter in perspective, the most popular Shakespeare quartos went through four or more editions over a period of several decades, whereas Sir Thomas Overbury's long moralizing poem *The Wife* went through five editions *in the first year of its publication alone*, 1614, and in ten editions before 1618.

Plays as Books

Transforming the text of a play into a book was not a straightforward process. A script is a set of instructions for performance—this term for the text of a play supplied to the actors apparently dates only from the late nineteenth century; it also implies that the work is written by hand. Nevertheless, turning the script into a performance involves not simply following instructions, but supplying a good deal of both action and interpretation—any play, by the time it reaches the stage, is a profoundly collaborative enterprise. Turning the play then into a reading text, a legible narrative, requires even more rethinking. A great deal of information is required in a narrative, ranging from the most basic, such as the characters' names, to very complex stage directions. Consider, for example, the king in *Hamlet*. Modern texts invariably call him Claudius, but his name is never mentioned in the play—in performance he is only the King. The name Claudius appears twice in the second quarto text and once in the folio, in a single stage direction for his first entrance: "*Enter Claudius King of Denmarke*"; in Q2 this is immediately followed by the speech heading *Claud*. In the folio the speech heading is simply *King*. Why is he named Claudius, then; for whose benefit is the name included? The answer can only be, for Shakespeare's. It is, then, not an element of performance, but part of the creative process, and it eventually became part of the reading process. And the dumb show preceding the play within the play, a long and complex action, is represented in the book only as a long stage direction.

The earliest surviving English secular drama (that is, one not part of a religious cycle), Henry Medwall's *Fulgens and Lucres* (c.1497) was printed by John Rastell sometime between 1511 and 1516; this is the first printed drama in England. The play had been composed as the entertainment for a banquet given by Cardinal John Morton, Archbishop of Canterbury; Medwall was a member of his household. The play is based on an Italian Renaissance dialogue that had been translated into English and published by William Caxton in 1481. It concerns the choice of a husband by Lucres, daughter of the noble Fulgens. Her two suitors are Publius Cornelius, a rich aristocrat but also a wastrel playboy, and the virtuous, high-minded Gayus, a commoner of modest but adequate means. Initially Lucres asks her father to choose for her, but he leaves the decision to her, and it is to her that the contenders make their appeal. To modern readers this sounds as if the case is loaded in favor of Gayus, but a sixteenth-century father might well have preferred an alliance with a rich aristocratic family to one that merely provides his daughter with a satisfactory husband.

The play is set in ancient Rome, but it includes three servants, comic characters from Medwall's contemporary world. The performance was in two parts, with the banquet in between. Two household attendants discuss the play, and then enter it, becoming the servants of the two suitors. One of them unsuccessfully woos Lucres's maid. In the dialogue the two attendants are never named; the maid is called Jone. But in the printed text the two attendants' speech headings call them A and B, and call the maid An. "An" may not be intended as her name, the modern Ann or Anne, but as an abbreviation of "Ancilla," maid; but the need for identification is a function of publication—the actors had received their parts and knew what roles they were playing, and for the purposes of performance names were unnecessary, especially since the attendants were (or were purporting to be) members of Cardinal Morton's household. They were in effect playing themselves.

So to begin with there was an editorial process to transform the play into a book: readers need to know who is speaking. The process is evident even in the earliest surviving manuscript of ancient drama, a palimpsest with a text of Plautus from the fourth or fifth century CE beneath a biblical text of the ninth century (this is known as the Ambrosian Palimpsest).[3] What is legible of the Plautus manuscript includes scene headings, the names of the characters in each scene, and who is speaking—these were obviously necessary for reading, but would not have been included in the parts supplied to the actors. At the same time, there appears to be no indication of when during a scene characters enter or depart, and no stage directions—reading the play still required a good deal of imagination to derive from it either a sense of performance or a narrative.

This manuscript is thought to have originally included all twenty-one of the plays ascribed to Plautus in late antiquity—earlier sources credit Plautus with 130 plays; similarly, Sophocles was said to have written 120 plays, of which only seven survive. Even if these are exaggerations, it is clear that a great many plays have been lost. For comparison, in the great age of Elizabethan, Jacobean, and Caroline theater, it is estimated that roughly three thousand plays would have been produced, of which 744 are identifiable by either the title or the name of the principal character, and the texts of 543 survive.[4] Theater was, by its nature, ephemeral; and there clearly was not, over time, a concerted effort to preserve it.

And yet, if Farmer and Lesser are correct, why would preserving and marketing plays not have been simply good business, as clearly, despite the more modest sales, marketing sermons was? But doubtless many more sermons than plays have been lost: There was a sermon every Sunday throughout the year, at every parish throughout the realm. Publishing books, even ones that promised to be profitable, was a complex matter; until late in the sixteenth century there was relatively little market for published plays, and preparing the

---

[3] Ms. Ambrosiano O 39 sup., now in the Bibliotheca Ambrosiana in Milan.
[4] The estimates, of course, vary by the sources taken into account. See the Lost Plays database, https://lostplays.folger.edu, and David McInnis and Matthew Steggle, eds, *Lost Plays in Shakespeare's England* (Houndsmill: Palgrave Macmillan, 2014).

manuscript of a play for the press was a great deal more complex than preparing the manuscript of a sermon. It is not even clear what we mean by the text of a play, the manuscript of which would have gone through various states in order to reach performance, from the draft which the playwright (or playwrights) delivered to the company, through their revisions, to the fair copy that was submitted to the Master of the Revels or the Lord Chamberlain for his certification that the play could indeed be performed, which might then become the prompter's copy, or the basis for it, to the individual parts distributed to the actors.[5] Any of these might be thought of as the text of the play. Barbara Mowat calls attention to persistent editorial misconceptions about the texts of Shakespeare, observing that "editors continue to debate which version prints *the* authorial manuscript and which *the* theatrical 'prompt-book,' or which prints the early holograph and which the holograph revision . . . [T]his clinging to illusions about 'prompt-books' and 'authorial manuscripts' . . . blinds us to the possibility that there may have been a large flow of manuscript copies of Shakespeare plays, copies marked by the idiosyncracies of manuscript transmission . . ."[6]

Preparing the play for print, rather than for performance, involved a different but equally complex set of revisions. The play in its initial quarto or octavo edition, moreover, was typically not identical to the play in any subsequent folio compilation, or in the various collected editions of the work of well-known playwrights, which increasingly included not only the regularization required by the conventions of printing, but in addition guides to the material for the reader's benefit—lists of characters, stage directions, act and scene divisions, and the like. Returning the play to the stage then involved a new set of revisions to address the needs of the actors and spectators rather than those of readers.

---

[5] Robert Weimann, *Author's Pen and Actor's Voice* (Cambridge: Cambridge University Press, 2000), Douglas Brooks, *From Playhouse to Printing House* (Cambridge: Cambridge University Press, 2000), and Paul Menzer, *The* Hamlets (Newark, DE: University of Delaware Press, 2008) give thoughtful discussions of the issues.

[6] Barbara Mowat, "The Problem of Shakespeare's Text(s)," in *Textual Formations and Reformations*, ed. Laurie Maguire and Thomas Berger (Newark, DE: University of Delaware Press, 1998), p. 136.

Tamburlaine

Consider the case of Marlowe's heroic drama *Tamburlaine*. The play opens with a Prologue announcing the inauguration of a new kind of theater, one that rejects "jygging vaines of riming mother wits" and "clownage"; but the published version of the play opens with an editorial preface that admits to the expurgation from the text of "fond and frivolous Jestures" and "deformities" that "have been of some vaine conceited fondlings greatly gaped at."[7] It is generally agreed that the Prologue is by Marlowe and formed part of the original staged script; if so, the "fond and frivolous Jestures" and "deformities" deplored in the preface were part of the author's original idea, part of the script. And though the Prologue disparages "clownage," apparently there was still too much of it in the play for the taste of the editor-publisher, who clearly believed that there had been some miscalculation on Marlowe's part, which he undertakes to correct in the printed text, in effect to bring the play into line with its own claims in the Prologue. It is surely relevant that in 1590, when the play's two parts were entered in the Stationers' Register, the record book that conferred permission to print, they were called "twooe comicall discourses"—the "fond and frivolous Jestures" and "clownage" were initially the determining feature of the play's genre. But the title page of the octavo published later the same year calls them "two Tragicall Discourses": When the play became literature it claimed a different decorum.

Obviously some editorial adjustment is going on here. It is of course also possible that the Prologue too is a feature of the printed copy, not of the original script, in which case the prose preface is simply a paraphrase of the Prologue. If that is not the case, however, then clearly Marlowe's notion of theatrical decorum differed from that of his editor—the book is not the play. In a printed drama, the audience's "conceited gaping" is not an issue, but that is only because their reactions are no longer part of the performance, so that they can in effect be ignored. A substantial part of *Doctor Faustus* consists of clownage, and the play has its share of fond and frivolous gestures. These are always now ascribed to a collaborator, but it sounds as if the original

---

[7] (London 1590), fol. A2^r.

Tamburlaine followed the same model. Perhaps, then, the Elizabethan stage was not transformed by Marlowe and *Tamburlaine* into something heroic and emotionally consistent at all; perhaps all that happened was that the script became a book and the book had an editor, and the essential transformation was not one of theatrical style, but the transformation of theater into print, and thereby the suppression or loss of an essential kind of performative energy, the energy of the audience.

Play versus Book

In short, watching a play in the period has little in common with reading a book. Playwrights invoked reliably popular generic elements to attract audiences—revenge, disguise, romance, history, current events—but the audience was an active and often unpredictable element of the play, and what happened in the course of any performance was only partly and intermittently determined by the script. Renaissance actors often improvised; Renaissance audiences always did—the practice is parodied in Francis Beaumont's *Knight of the Burning Pestle* (performed 1607, published 1613). Richard Preiss in a brilliant and extensive discussion of improvisation on the Renaissance stage cites a number of cases in which the spectators interrupted and even re-directed the play.[8] The anecdotes are hilarious, outrageous, and without exception unverifiable; they may be entirely fictional, early modern urban legends. It is significant, however, that they all imagine an audience with agency—that is the way audiences were imagined. The play, in these accounts, is not merely its text, it is a fraught social event. Moreover, the consequence of publication is the stabilization of the play's text, whereas in performance the play keeps changing, not simply because every iteration will differ to some degree from every other one, but because performance takes the audience into account; the play before the king was not the same as the play at the Globe, and neither of these was the play at the more demotic Red Bull or the more elite Blackfriars. Acting companies always change what they perform as tastes and audiences change.

---

[8] "What Audiences Did," the opening chapter of Preiss's book *Clowning and Authorship in Early Modern Theatre* (Cambridge: Cambridge University Press, 2014).

William Proctor Williams gives a very clear sense both of how far the performing text was from whatever the playwright gave the actors, and of how far the actors' version was from the version that eventually became a book:

> The playwright(s) produced, eventually, a draft which then underwent some further revision so that another draft needed to be produced, clean enough for the Master of the Revels to read and understand; and from that came what was known as the Approved Book (those manuscripts with the Master of the Revels' authority to play inscribed somewhere on them) which may have been the same as the previous draft but could have been yet a further draft; and from that came yet another document we have come to call the Promptbook; and from that or those almost certainly came further partial or whole manuscripts of the play; and all that adds up to four or five documents of various kinds just to get to performance with no notion of what will be required to get to print... About 800 plays have survived in print [the Lost Plays database, as we have seen, gives the much lower figure of 543], and between eighteen, twenty-one, and about 125 survive in some sort of manuscript (the difference in the numbers has to do with how dramatic manuscript is defined) but less than half these manuscripts are in any way connected to a printed edition, and, finally, no example of printer's copy survives for any of these plays.[9]

The difference between the book and the play increased over time. The eighteenth century saw the most concerted effort before the present to establish a correct text of Shakespeare; there was a new scholarly edition every ten years or so. All these differed from each other to some extent, but all their texts, even those that were based on previous editions, derived ultimately from sources that were taken to be original; and all regularized the text and corrected what were taken to be errors. Throughout the century Shakespeare in the theater, however, bore little resemblance to Shakespeare in the library: *The Tempest* was performed in Davenant and Dryden's adaptation, which includes less than a third of Shakespeare's text; and Davenant's romanticized version of *Macbeth* was, until Garrick, what one saw in the theater.

---

[9] William Proctor Williams, "What's a Lost Play?" in *Lost Plays in Shakespeare's England*, ed. David McInnis and Matthew Steggle (Houndsmill: Palgrave Macmillan, 2014), pp. 17–30. See also Tiffany Stern, "Plays in the Stationers' Register in the Time of Shakespeare" (2017). Web publication/site, Adam Matthew. http://www.literaryprintculture.amdigital.co.uk.

But in 1744 Garrick advertised his *Macbeth* as being performed, for the first time, as written by Shakespeare. The claim, however, was not even approximately true; all that was true was that Garrick took as his working text Lewis Theobald's recent edition of Shakespeare rather than the standard stage version of Davenant. But he cut more than 10 percent of this very short play, including the drunken porter, the murder of Macduff's son, and the dialogue in which Malcolm tests Macduff by imputing monstrous vices to himself. Authenticity in these cases was trumped by the good taste of the period, epitomized in a desire to tone down what were seen as the play's excesses. However, Garrick also retained some of Davenant's most popular bits for the witches, and wrote a whole new dying speech of his own for Macbeth. The original text was only marginally more satisfactory to Garrick's sense of the drama than it had been to Davenant's. Why then the claim of authenticity? Twenty years earlier a theater could have expected to attract audiences by advertising a wholly new *Macbeth*, bigger and better. Garrick's invocation of the author to confer authority on the production marks a significant moment in both theatrical and textual history.

The immense length of the standard printed texts of *Hamlet* (those in the second quarto and folio) always had to be cut for performance (though perhaps not for performances at court, which were typically much longer than those in the public playhouses),[10] and in the popular theater the play was always cut differently. The book in this case was not the performing text, but both were "Shakespeare." It is customary for us now to refer to the book of a play as the play—G. B. Shaw, Tennessee Williams, Samuel Beckett, or Arthur Miller plays are certainly books as well as theater pieces; and the stage directions are sometimes little essays designed to direct and limit interpretation. But even for modern works, a great deal of revision is required to transform a play script into a book, and any effort to return the printed text to performance—even if the performance is reading it aloud—will necessarily be at the very least an interpretation, and often another revision.

Legal opinion in Shakespeare's time was quite clear on the subject: in 1610 a group of players in Yorkshire were arrested and charged with sedition. Their offense was performing *Pericles*, *King Lear*, and a lost play about Saint George that the authorities claimed were (or perhaps had

---

[10] Richard Dutton argues that most of our Shakespeare texts, which are typically too long for the popular stage, were in fact prepared for performances at court. See *Shakespeare, Court Dramatist* (Oxford: Oxford University Press, 2016).

had introduced into them) Roman Catholic propaganda—the members of the troupe were Catholic. In their defense the actors replied that their performing texts of *Pericles* and *King Lear* were the published quartos. Since these had been duly licensed for publication they could not be considered seditious. This was not, however, considered a sufficient defense: the court took the position that the licensing of books is a different matter from the licensing of play scripts. Plays are social events involving crowds, and are therefore much more dangerous than individual readers or family groups. Books in 1610 were not plays. To argue that in modern usage a book may be a play is to acknowledge how much our sense of theater has changed.

Indeed, one can see the change taking place by the mid-seventeenth century. The publisher Humphrey Moseley's prefatory epistle to the Beaumont and Fletcher folio, issued in 1647, when the public theaters had by law been closed for five years, declares that the volume preserves "All that was *Acted*, and all that was not; even the perfect full Originalls without the least mutilation."[11] The perfect, full original here is only the text; what any performance does, according to Moseley, is mutilate it. The editors of the Shakespeare first folio had declared that their texts superseded the "stol'n and surreptitious," unauthorized and therefore inaccurate, texts in circulation. Mosely's claim goes a large step beyond this; the very fact that performance leaves some of the text unspoken, that the texts of plays are typically cut for public performance, is taken to be a form of mutilation. But the epistle is also written with a full sense that the text itself is only partial, all that remains of an ephemeral art "*in this* Tragicall *Age, where the Theater hath been so much out-acted.*"[12]

Enter the Playwright

Moseley's preface also signals a radical change from the previous generations' theater: the playwright has become central to how the drama is conceived, and the authority of the text is certified by its derivation

---

[11] *Comedies and Tragedies Written by Francis Beaumont and John Fletcher* (London, 1647), fol. A4^v.
[12] *Comedies and Tragedies* (1647), fol. A3^r.

directly from the author. This is only partly a consequence of the closing of the theaters in 1642. Until the late 1590s, the playwright was a distinctly marginal figure in the supremely collaborative enterprise of Elizabethan theater. Playwrights' names were not normally noted when plays were cited, and were rarely included on the title pages of published plays. Shakespeare's name first appears on the title page of a play in 1598, by which time he had been writing popular drama for seven or eight years, and his name had appeared in the very successful published editions of *Venus and Adonis* and *Lucrece* (though not on their title pages). What the title pages of his plays advertise instead is the acting company, and thereby the name of its aristocratic patron. *Tamburlaine* was an extremely popular play, constantly revived, published four times before 1604, but Marlowe's name was not definitively attached to it until well into the nineteenth century.

By the second decade of the seventeenth century, however, playwrights were beginning both to claim their work and to claim rights over its publication. Thomas Heywood, in a prefatory epistle to his defense of the stage *An Apology for Actors* (1612), notes the unauthorized inclusion of two of his translations from Ovid's *Heroides* in a new edition of the poetic anthology *The Passionate Pilgrim*, with the translations ascribed, moreover, to Shakespeare; and in the preface to his play *The Brazen Age* (1613), complains of the piracy of other of his translations from Ovid's love books. He certainly feels proprietary about these works; but like most early commentators on the subject, he appears to be ultimately more concerned about inferior work being credited to him, or to any author, than about his work being credited to others—Heywood claims that when his poetry was published under Shakespeare's name, Shakespeare was so indignant that he refused to have further dealings with the publisher (who was, ironically, William Jaggard, printer of the first folio).[13]

Heywood's examples were not plays, but in the "Advice to the Reader" of his play *The Rape of Lucrece* he explains his unwillingness to publish his plays: "some have used a double sale of their labours, first to the Stage and after to the Presse: For my owne part, I here proclaim my selfe

---

[13] For an excellent overview, see Max W. Thomas, "Eschewing Credit: Heywood, Shakespeare, and Plagiarism before Copyright," *New Literary History*, 31.2 (Spring, 2000), 277–93.

ever faithfull in the first, and never guilty of the last: yet since some of my Playes have (unknowne to me, and without any of my direction) accidentally come into the Printers hands, and therefore so corrupt and mangled, (copied onely by the eare) that I have been unable to know them, as ashamed to challenge them. This therefore I was the willinger to furnish out in his native habit . . ."[14] It has been doubted that there was any shorthand system at the time capable of recording a play, but Heywood's testimony is surely sufficient—sufficient also to indicate how inexact the transcription inevitably was. There were in fact, however, ten systems of shorthand published in England between 1588 and 1626, and Tiffany Stern has provided ample evidence of audiences taking notes at theater, not necessarily in shorthand.[15] Clearly there was a market for plays, even corrupt and mangled ones; and soon enough plays were being treated as literary property. The "bad" first quarto of *Hamlet* even includes passages marked with double quotes, which Peter Stallybrass and Zachary Lesser identify as commonplacing marks, excerptable bits of wisdom for readers to take special note of (the play here being treated as a literary text), though Stern offers an alternative theory that the double quotes, on the contrary, may indicate passages that were in fact omitted in some performances—the printed text, in this argument, would be made up of written reports by several different auditors at different times.[16] In either case, the text in the book is different from what one heard in the theater.

John Marston was a notably successful playwright in the late 1590s and the early years of the seventeenth century, writing primarily for the children's companies. By 1609 he had left the stage and entered holy orders, and wrote no more for the theater. However, in 1633, when he had been a clergyman for 24 years, the publisher William Sheares

---

[14] Thomas Heywood, *The Rape of Lucrece* (1608), fol. A2^r.

[15] Tiffany Stern's detailed argument is in "Sermons, Plays and Note-Takers: Hamlet Q1 as a 'Noted' Text," *Shakespeare Survey*, 66 (2013), 1–23. See also the discussion of the transcription of plays by auditors (the examples are for the most part Spanish and French) by Roger Chartier, *Publishing Drama in Early Modern Europe* (The Panizzi Lectures, London: The British Library, 1999), pp. 28–46.

[16] See Zachary Lesser and Peter Stallybrass, "The First Literary *Hamlet* and the Commonplacing of Professional Plays," *Shakespeare Quarterly*, 59.4 (2008), 371–420. See also Carla Suthren, "Translating Commonplacing Marks in Gascoigne and Kinwelmersh's *Jocasta*," *Translation and Literature*, 29.1 (March 2020), 59–84. Stern's counter-argument is in "Sermons, Plays and Note-Takers," p. 20.

issued a collection of six of his comedies and tragedies with a dedication to Elizabeth Cary, Lady Falkland. The dedication was provided by the publisher—Marston was clearly not involved—but Marston must have objected to the volume, since in the same year the edition was reissued with a new title page from which his name had been removed. All the interior title pages, which also included his name (or in one case his initials) were removed simply by being sliced out of the remaining copies (the printers were inefficient at this, and copies survive with the new title page and the original internal title pages intact). Perhaps Lady Falkland also objected, since the leaves with the dedication to her were also removed. Though Marston did not own the rights to his plays, he clearly felt a strong proprietary interest in them. His connections were not powerful enough to force the outright suppression of the book, but he succeeded in having his association with it suppressed.

At this period published drama also starts to look more like literature, including not only authors' names but dedications, lists of characters, and other prefatory material, sometimes with commendatory verses; and a more formalized text, often (but not invariably) divided into acts and scenes, and from about 1590 in roman type rather than the traditional English gothic type, now called black letter, but in the period called simply english. The new style was modeled on French and Italian editions of the Roman dramatists, and was recognized as classical. From the late sixteenth century it had been the normal style for English plays not designed for the public playhouse (what came to be called "Closet Drama," for the most part plays by aristocrats, e.g., the Countess of Pembroke's *Antonie*, 1592, or *Antonius*, 1595, a translation from the French of Robert Garnier) and for plays that were presented as prestigious (e.g., Kyd's classical tragedy *Cornelia*, 1594, in roman type, but not the very popular tragicomedy *Cambises*, 1570, reprinted 1595, with its clowning intact and still in black letter), but by the early seventeenth century it was for the most part the format for all new drama. Popular old plays, however, retained the old look; thus, as late as 1631 Marlowe's *Doctor Faustus* was reissued in black letter, and with no acts and scenes.[17]

---

[17] Claire Bourne's *Typographies of Performance in Early Modern England* (Oxford: Oxford University Press, 2020) gives a compendious and thoughtful account of the developing look of early English printed drama.

2

The Example of *Gorboduc*

Gorboduc was the first Elizabethan play to achieve a kind of classic status, a tragedy about a legendary king of Britain who (according to the historian Geoffrey of Monmouth), in order to preclude dissension after his death, divides his kingdom between his two sons Ferrex and Porrex—Gorboduc was the grandson or great-grandson of King Lear, and replays his tragedy. As in Shakespeare's *King Lear*, the result is instead hostility between the children, and resultant civil war. The work was written by Thomas Norton and Thomas Sackville, two members of the law society the Inner Temple, and presented before the young Queen Elizabeth I shortly after her ascent to the throne; it was designed as a warning to the unmarried queen without children about the importance of ensuring a secure succession. *Gorboduc* is frequently cited for various kinds of priority: it is the first English "regular" drama (that is, on a classical model), the first to include dumb shows (pantomime interludes), the first in blank verse, the first with a contemporary political subject. But in fact, none of these claims can be substantiated. *Gorboduc* is only the first *published* play with these characteristics. Of the multitude of earlier entertainments that were not preserved in print, we can say nothing. But every aristocratic banquet had an entertainment, often a play, and there were civic pageants, cycle plays, and private theatricals, including many at court. Modern studies of English drama regularly take as their earliest significant landmark the founding of the first public theater in London in 1576,[1] but this date is entirely arbitrary: historically most post-classical theater until at least late Elizabethan times, even professional theater, was itinerant and was not dependent on the dedicated real estate of purpose-built theaters.[2] In fact, the appearance of *Gorboduc* as a book was unusual, even anomalous, having more to do with its aristocratic authors and direct address to the queen than with any market for printed drama.

What the Audience Saw

It is clear, moreover, that the printed text of *Gorboduc* is quite different from the play the earliest audiences saw. Greg Walker and Henry James have called attention to a contemporary account of the first performance at Christmas 1560, at the Inns of Court, followed several weeks later at Whitehall with the queen in attendance:

> Ther was a Tragedie played in the Inner Temple of the two brethren Porrex and Ferrex K[ings] of Brytayne betwene whome the father had devyded the Realme, the one slewe the other and the mother slewe the manquil[e]r [i.e., the manqueller or man-killer]. It was thus used. Firste wilde men cam[e] in and woulde have broken a whole fagott, but could not, the stickes they brake being severed [this was the first dumb show]. Then cam[e] in a king to whome was geven a clere glasse, and a golden cupp of golde covered, full of poyson, the glasse he caste under his fote and brake hyt, the poyson he drank of [this was the second dumb show], after cam[e] in mom[m]ers [the fourth dumb show]. The shadowes [i.e., dumb shows] were declared by the Chor[us] first to signyfie unytie, the 2 [second] howe that men refused the certen and toocke the uncerten, wherby was ment that yt was better for the Quene to marye L[ord] R[obert] Dudley, subsequently Earl of Leicester] knowen then with the K[ing] of Sweden. The thryde to declare that cyvill discention bredeth mo[u]rning. Many thinges were handled of mariage, and that the matter was to

---

[1] It was called simply The Theatre, thus asserting both its priority and its uniqueness. An earlier purpose-built playhouse, The Red Lion, constructed in 1567 in Whitechapel (just east of the city of London) for John Brayne, the brother-in-law of James Burbage (for whom The Theatre was built), apparently survived for only a year.

[2] For an excellent account of itinerant theater see Richard Dutton, *Shakespeare, Court Dramatist* (Oxford: Oxford University Press, 2016), pp. 14–27.

be debated in p[ar]liament, because yt was much banding [very contentious] but th[at] hit ought to be determined by the councell. Ther was also declared howe a straunge duke seying the realme at dyvysion, would have taken upon him the crowne, but the people would none of hytt. And many thinges were saied for the succession to put thinges in certenty.[3]

In this account, the meaning of the play is conveyed through its dumb shows, interludes without dialogue that presented symbolic commentary on the action. In the published texts each of the acts is preceded by a pantomime; in this account only three of the dumb shows are described, and all precede the whole drama. This may reflect only the reporter's method of summarizing; but it is significant that meaning here is conveyed not by the dialogue and action, but by the dumb shows and choruses—this version of *Gorboduc* sounds more like a traditional mummers' play, with its disguise and pantomime, than like a classical drama.

But more strikingly, the account of the dumb shows is quite different from the dumb shows described in the published text. As we read *Gorboduc*, the play's meaning is quite general, having to do with keeping the commonwealth intact through securing the succession should the monarch die without issue. But for this spectator at the original performance, its meaning was quite specific. The queen was being counseled to marry her domestic suitor Robert Dudley, not the foreign suitor, the king of Sweden. The interpretation of the second dumb show in particular differs significantly from that given in the printed text. When our spectator saw the play, the Chorus explained the contrast of a clear glass and a golden cup as being about marriage with the known versus the unknown; whereas in the printed text, the Chorus says it is about good counsel versus flattery. Marriage is not an issue anywhere in the play as it was published; but at the original performance, "Many thinges were handled of mariage." The book we have was not the play the first audiences saw.[4]

---

[3] Henry James and Greg Walker, "The Politics of *Gorboduc*," *English Historical Review*, 110.435 (February 1995), 109–21.

[4] For the full discussion, from which this is taken, see my *Wit's Treasury* (Philadelphia: University of Pennsylvania Press, 2021), pp. 131–2.

By the time the play was published, the king of Sweden was no longer a suitor for the queen's hand, and public discussion of the queen's marriage prospects was forbidden. Thus the text would have been thoroughly revised to be approved for publication. And in fact the second edition of the play, published by John Day in 1570 under the title *The Tragidie of Ferrex and Porrex*, claims both to have corrected numerous errors in the earlier text, and also to be "set forth without addition or alteration but altogether as the same was shewed on stage before the Queenes Majestie." Both these claims are demonstrably false: Day's text is clearly based on the earlier one, including all its revisions; the new edition also underwent some additional censorship. It was not at all the play as performed before Elizabeth. But the claim of an updated and approved text is not conceived to be a selling point. The market is assumed to consist of buyers who want what the queen saw.

Other Examples

By the 1590s, however, the facts of revision and a fuller text than you could experience in performance had become selling points for books of plays. Thus the printed text of *Tamburlaine* announces its expurgation of "fond and frivolous Jestures" and "deformities," and the second quarto of *Hamlet* declares on its title page that it is "enlarged to almost as much againe as it was, according to the true and perfect Coppie"—the true and perfect (i.e., correct and complete) copy was far longer than the previous edition, the first quarto, which was the right length for a play in the public theater and was clearly some version of what was actually being staged.[5] The market for published plays had changed; the attraction of the book was now that it gave you something more or better than the play in the theater.

We are still a long way from Humphrey Moseley's assumption that the *real* play was the author's text, "all that was acted and all that was not,"

---

[5] While the first quarto of *Hamlet* cannot simply be the script, it is much closer to the realities of the stage than either Q2 or the folio texts, providing real detail about the play in performance: e.g., when the Ghost appears in the Queen's bedroom he is said to be *"in his night gowne"* (fol. G2^v)—in modern productions he is invariably still in the armor of his first appearance, quite inappropriately for a visit to a bedroom; Ophelia in her mad scene is *"playing on a Lute, and her haire downe"* (fol. G4^v).

and that performance mutilates the original; but Ben Jonson's complaint that the actors had "never acted but most negligently played" his late comedy *The New Inn* (1629) and were responsible for its failure in the theater is clearly a precedent for Moseley's attitude. Jonson very consciously took possession of the texts of his plays, not only revising but adding a good deal of paratextual material and seeing them through the press, so that the text became an address to an audience of readers, without the mediation of actors—ironically, since Jonsonian comedy relies so heavily on a troupe of virtuoso actors. The comedy of humors (in which each character is dominated by a particular personality trait, determined by an imbalance of the "humors," the bodily fluids that, according to ancient psychology, regulate our behavior) is always described as a comedy of types, but the casts of *The Alchemist*, *Volpone*, *Bartholomew Fair* need to be a group of brilliant comedians with their individual routines. In his dedicatory epistle, Jonson refers to *The Alchemist* as a poem, thereby eliding the actors. But when he blames the actors for the failure of *The New Inn* he is acknowledging how much he has made depend on the performers.

There are precedents within Jonson's own age for the elision of the actors from theater. Consider Thomas Nashe's praise of Shakespeare's depiction of the hero John Talbot, Earl of Shrewsbury, in 1 *Henry VI*:

> How would it have joyed brave *Talbot* (the terror of the French) to thinke that after he had lyne two hundred yeares in his Tombe, hee should triumphe againe on the Stage, and have his bones newe embalmed with the teares of ten thousand spectators at least, (at severall times) who in the Tragedian that represents his person, imagine they behold him fresh bleeding.[6]

The tragedian here is both an afterthought and anonymous; all the praise is for the character, the plot, the story. (In contrast, a modern critic who wrote of the excitement of seeing Queen Elizabeth I brought to life on screen would have been calling attention to the talents of the actor, Cate Blanchette or Judi Dench.) There is classical precedent for Jonson's attitude as well—Aristotle's treatise about transforming a ritualized spectacle into rules for drama is, after all, *The Poetics*, not something like *The Histrionics* or *The Theatrics*.

---

[6] Thomas Nashe, *Pierce Penilesse his Supplication to the Divell* (1592), fol. F3r.

Thomas Kyd's *The Spanish Tragedy*, which was very popular both in the theater and in print, is explicit about the competing claims of stage and book. Written sometime in the 1580s (but presumably before 1588, since it makes no reference to the defeat of the Spanish Armada), it was revised and new scenes were added for productions within about a decade. Philip Henslowe notes that in 1601 Ben Jonson was paid for "writtinge of his adicians in geronimo" (the play is cited by the name of its central character Hieronymo); eight months later Jonson was paid again "for newe adicyons to Jeronymo,"[7] and an updated version of the play was published in 1602. The play in these two versions was published eleven times by 1633. The title pages of the earliest editions make a specifically editorial claim:

> Newly corrected and amended of such grosse faults as passed in the first impression.

Thus the title page of the earliest surviving edition, 1592—no copy of that first impression survives (of the 1592 edition, only a single copy is known). Editions after 1602, which include the theatrical revisions, invoke the play's popularity on stage:

> Newly corrected, amended, and enlarged with new additions of the Painters part, and others, as it hath been of late divers times acted.

And yet the text acknowledges that it has been revised explicitly for readers. When Hieronimo prepares his murderous play within the play, he produces a text in many languages.

> *Hieronimo.* Each one of us must act his parte,
> In unknowne languages,
> That it may breede the more varietie.

Despite Balthazar's objection, "But this will be a meere confusion, | And hardly shall we all be understoode,"[8] that is how the play was performed. But a note in the printed text reads:

---

[7] See Lukas Erne, *Beyond* The Spanish Tragedy (Revels Plays Companion Library, Manchester: Manchester University Press, 1988), pp. 119–20.

[8] Thomas Kyd, *The Spanish Tragedy* (1592), fol. K1^v.

> Gentlemen, this play of Hieronimo, in sundrie Languages, was thought good to be set downe in English more largely, for the easier understanding to every publique Reader.⁹

The "publique reader" has become the audience (and is assumed to be male—for the book, the large female component of both the theater audience and the library has been elided). As for the "new additions ... of late divers times acted," Lukas Erne observes that "they were in all probability designed as replacements rather than additions."¹⁰ The editors of the recent Arden edition agree.¹¹ Erne considers it doubtful that the printed additions are the ones for which Jonson was paid—aside from the stylistic difficulties, he was paid in 1601 and 1602, and there is evidence that the new material was being performed by 1599.¹²

This famous and very popular play was, then, significantly revised over the years for performance, but also, and differently, for publication. Erne notes that "by the time [the additions] came to be written, Jonson, Marston, and Donne had made their débuts and the style of the dramatisation of Hieronimo's grief and madness must have seemed decidedly out of date."¹³ The revisions as they were printed are somewhat garbled, obviously missing lines and phrases; but they are certainly much freer in style, much more "modern," than the original text. Nothing of Donne's had been published by 1602, so updating the play with poetry that sounded like Donne suggests at the very least a quite sophisticated reviser (and audience); it might also suggest an audience of readers. There is some evidence for ascribing the added Painter's scene to Marston, but nothing in Jonson sounds at all like the additions to the old tragedy. Anne Barton and David Riggs work hard to connect the new material with Jonson, citing the death of his infant daughter Mary in 1601 as providing a model for Hieronimo's grief at the murder of his son Horatio, but the analogy is far-fetched, and in any case the performing revisions seem to have been in existence

---

⁹ Kyd, *Spanish Tragedy*, fol. K3ʳ.
¹⁰ *Beyond* The Spanish Tragedy, p. 123.
¹¹ Thomas Kyd, *The Spanish Tragedy*, ed. Clara Calvo and Jesus Tronch (Arden Early Modern Drama, London: Bloomsbury, 2013), p. 27n.1.
¹² *Beyond* The Spanish Tragedy, pp. 121–2.
¹³ *Beyond* The Spanish Tragedy, p. 124.

two years earlier. Brian Vickers's and Douglas Bruster's stylometric and orthographic research have produced a case for Shakespeare as the reviser.[14] The very expert Tiffany Stern considers the case a strong but inconclusive one.[15]

The Drama of Editing

Even when the play was not revised for publication, translating the conventions of manuscript into those of print was not a straightforward matter. Consider the basic issue of whether a passage is prose or verse.[16] This is an issue that will be of much more significance to editors and typographers than to actors, who will speak the passage as they see fit, however it is presented in writing. Here, from *The Tempest*, is a speech of Caliban's interrupted by a remark of Trinculo's as it appears in the folio—the folio preserves our only text. Except for a single line, Caliban's speeches are set as prose, but have been, since Pope's edition (1723–25), printed as verse:

> *Cal.* I'le shew thee the best springs: I'le plucke thee Berries: I'le fish for thee; and get thee wood enough.
> A plague upon the Tyrant that I serve;
> I'le bear him no more Stickes, but follow thee, thou wondrous man.
> *Tri.* A most ridiculous Monster, to make a wonder of a poore drunkard.
> *Cal.* I'prethee let me bring thee where Crabs grow; and I with my long nayles will digge thee pig-nuts; show thee a Jayes nest, and instruct thee how to snare the nimble Marmazet: I'le bring thee to

---

[14] Brian Vickers, "Identifying Shakespeare's Additions to *The Spanish Tragedy* (1602): A New(er) Approach," *Shakespeare*, 8.1 (2012), 13–43; Douglas Bruster, "Shakespearean Spellings and Handwriting in the Additional Passages Printed in the 1602 *Spanish Tragedy*," *Notes and Queries*, 60 (2013), 420–4.

[15] Stern, according to *The New York Times*, "praised the empirical rigor of Mr. Bruster's paper, but said that some new attributions were driven less by solid evidence than by publishers' desire to offer 'more Shakespeare' than their rivals. The arguments for 'The Spanish Tragedy' are better than for most putative Shakespeare collaborations, Ms. Stern said. 'But I think we're going a bit Shakespeare-attribution crazy and shoving a lot of stuff in that maybe shouldn't be there.'" "Much Ado About Shakespeare," August 12, 2013, Section A, p. 1.

[16] For the full argument see my essay "Acting Scripts, Performing Texts," in my collection *The Authentic Shakespeare and Other Problems of the Early Modern Stage* (New York: Routledge, 2002), pp. 21–48.

clustring Philberts, and sometimes I'le get thee young Scamels
from the Rocke: Wilt thou go with me?

(2.2.154–66)

Pope took Caliban's lines to be "really" verse because metrically they can be construed that way, and all subsequent editors have concurred; but why do we treat them as verse rather than as prose that has the rhythm of verse? Clearly some judgment about the true nature of Caliban's language, and thereby of Caliban's character, is involved. Conversely, a group of verse speeches by Stephano in 3.2 have since Pope just as obviously appeared to be prose:

> *Trinculo*, if you trouble him any more in's tale,
> By this hand, I will supplant some of your teeth.
> ...
> How now shall this be compast?
> Canst thou bring me to the party?
> ...
> Do I so? Take thou that,
> As you like this, give me the lye another time.
> ...
> Give me thy hand, I am sorry I beate thee:
> But while thou liv'st keepe a good tongue in thy head.
> ...
> At thy request Monster, I will do reason,
> Any reason: Come on *Trinculo*, let us sing.

Here is the final exchange in the scene between the three conspirators as the folio prints it:

> *Ste*. This will prove a brave kingdome to me,
> Where I shall have my Musicke for nothing.
>   *Cal.* When *Prospero* is destroy'd.
>   *Ste*. That shall be by and by:
> I remember the storie.
>   *Trin*. The sound is going away,
> Lets follow it, and after do our worke.
>   *Ste*. Leade Monster,
> Wee'l follow: I would I could see this Taborer,
> He layes it on.
>   *Trin*. Wilt come?
> Ile follow *Stephano*.   *Exeunt*.

(3.2.142–50)

The layout of the verse passages has been explained by the compositor's purported need to lose space at the end of the scene, though no editor who subscribes to this explanation has gone on to consider the implications of the assumption that in 1623 Shakespeare's prose could become verse for reasons that had nothing to do with either authorial intention or metrics. But no compositorial exigencies will account for the folio setting of a speech of Stephano's in Act 5, which since Pope has invariably been printed as prose:

> *Ste.* Every man shift for all the rest, and let
> No man take care for himselfe; for all is
> But fortune: *Coragio* Bully-Monster *Corasio* [sic].
>
> (5.1.256–8)

Why do we declare this to be prose, rather than inept poetry?

If the question seems perverse in the face of what seem such clear-cut examples, let us turn to a case that looks (though not, on the whole, to editors) less clear-cut, and where the question will look more like a real one. What shall we do about a passage in the opening storm scene on the ship that the folio prints this way:

> Though every drop of water sweare against it,
> And gape at widst to glut him.   *A confused noyse within.*
> Mercy on us.
> We split, we split, Farewell my wife, and children,
> Farewell brother: we split, we split, we split.
>
> (1.1.58–63)

The stage direction declares what follows to be "a confused noise": Can a confused noise be blank verse? Editors have consistently answered yes. Pope believed not only that this was verse, but also that it must originally have been better verse than it is: he regularized the final line to "Brother farewell, we split, we split, we split."

Edward Capell, in his Shakespeare edition of 1767–68, was the first editor to perceive a difficulty, and printed the whole passage as a stage direction, with the clauses separated by dashes—as confused noise, that is. This seemingly sensible emendation, however, failed to persuade the majority of subsequent editors, who almost without exception have adhered to the folio lineation.

Antony and Cleopatra[17] provides a reverse instance. Here, from the folio, is an exchange between Cleopatra and the messenger who brings the news of Antony's marriage to Octavia:

> *Mes.* Most gracious Majestie.
> *Cleo.* Did'st thou behold *Octavia*?
> *Mes.* I dread Queene.
> *Cleo.* Where?
> *Mes.* Madam in Rome, I lookt her in the face: and saw her led betweene her Brother, and *Marke Anthony*.

Since the Johnson-Steevens-Reed edition of 1793, the passage has almost invariably been printed like this:

> *Mes.* Most gracious majesty—
> *Cleo.*   Didst thou behold Octavia?
> *Mes.*   Ay, dread queen.
> *Cleo.*   Where?
> *Mes.*   Madam, in Rome.
> I look'd her in the face; and saw her led
> Between her brother and Mark Antony.
>
> (3.3.7–10)

What is involved in deciding that such examples are "really" not verse but prose, or not prose but verse? The cases of the confused noise and Cleopatra's exchange with the messenger clearly conceive the playhouse as either a contaminating medium or as simply irrelevant: editors have decided with overwhelming unanimity that however the drowning sailors, Cleopatra, and the messenger, will deliver their lines, they are nevertheless speaking blank verse. There is an editorial syllogism with strong moral overtones at work here: it says that verse is better than prose, Shakespeare is the best poet, and therefore anything that can be rendered as proper verse should be. As for Caliban's blank verse and Stephano's and Trinculo's prose, these may seem to have more to do with judgments about stylistic consistency, but here too, it is doubtful

---

[17] In the folios the name is Anthonie or Anthony (in *Julius Caesar* it is Antony; in North's Plutarch it is Antony or Antonie). Since Rowe's edition of 1709, it has been modernized to Antony throughout the play.

that their underlying assumptions are merely metrical. They are moral and even political, having to do with how we want their speakers to be perceived. Caliban has been systematically ennobled by representing his prose as verse wherever possible—even as Prospero's character has been sweetened and sentimentalized by the critical tradition, the editorial tradition has tended to take Caliban's side against him; Caliban does, after all, have some of the most beautiful language in the play. Conversely, Stephano and Trinculo are presented as too vulgar and inconsequential for verse, even for doggerel. But more deeply, the editorial assumptions have to do with issues of Shakespeare's own nature: *Can* the greatest poet have written doggerel? Didn't he really, most of the time, *think* in blank verse?

In *Julius Caesar*, Brutus and Mark Antony deliver funeral orations after the murder of Caesar. Brutus's is very formal Ciceronian prose, Antony's in blank verse. Antony's is the more effective; but the problem with Brutus's speech is not that it is in prose—Brutus elsewhere speaks verse—but that it is clearly a studied performance, and to that extent unfeeling. The plain speakers here speak verse—Cicero himself, the model for classical prose, in his few lines in the play speaks blank verse; and though Casca's account of Antony offering Caesar the crown is prose, he elsewhere speaks verse.

Verse and Prose

A number of theatrical manuscripts have survived from the period. These are the sort of texts the folio compositors would have been working from, and they render modern assumptions about verse and prose very suspect. What kind of evidence have we about the distinction between verse and prose in Shakespeare's time? *The Tempest* and several other Shakespeare plays were prepared for the press by the scrivener Ralph Crane, many of whose transcriptions survive. In these, it is not always clear whether a given passage is prose or verse; Crane did not make much of a distinction between them. Was this a transcriber's idiosyncracy, or does it reflect a feature of the manuscripts he was copying? There is no Shakespeare holograph for us to compare with the folio text of *The Tempest*,[18] but Crane made three copies of Thomas

---

[18] A section of the collaborative play *Sir Thomas More*, composed in the 1590s and which exists in manuscript, is widely considered to be in Shakespeare's hand, but the

Middleton's violently anti-Spanish and very popular play *A Game at Chesse* (1624), of which one manuscript in Middleton's own hand and another partly in his hand also survive. In Middleton's texts, as in Crane's, the form is often ambiguous; the most familiar prosodic marker of verse to us, capitals at the beginning of lines, is absent in all copies—such capitalization was essentially a printing convention, not a manuscript one, and R. C. Bald's edition of Middleton's complete holograph misrepresents the manuscript by substituting initial capitals for what he takes to be verse throughout, thereby removing the ambiguity.[19] The following passage, however, looks unambiguously like verse in Crane's texts:

> *Black Pawn.* They'd need have given you a whole bag by yourself.
> 'Sfoot! This Fat Black Bishop has so squelched and squeezed me,
> So overlaid me, I have no verjuice Left in me. You shall find all my goodness
>   If you look for't, in the bottom of the bag.
>
>   (5.3.187–91)[20]

But in both Middleton's holographs the passage is just as unambiguously prose (see figure 2.1; the passage begins at line 7).

Nevertheless, it is, predictably, printed as verse in both Bald's and Gary Taylor's more recent authoritative editions. For these editors, not even the evidence of two autograph manuscripts outweighs the prejudice in favor of verse.

Let us now consider an alternative example. A manuscript of the play in the Huntington Library is partly in a scribe's hand and partly in Middleton's.

Figure 2.2 shows the scribe rendering a passage that must be prose, a letter being read aloud. The passage begins near the bottom of the left-hand page, and is labeled, at the far right, "The Letter." In its arrangement on the page it is indistinguishable from verse. The layout cannot be accounted for by proposing that the scribe did not know he was transcribing prose: the passage is explicitly indicated as a letter, and

---

case remains inconclusive, and has been persuasively challenged by Paul Werstine, "Shakespeare, *More* or Less: A. W. Pollard and Twentieth-Century Shakespeare Editing," *Florilegium*, 16 (1999), 25–45.

[19] Thomas Middleton, *A Game at Chesse*, ed. R. C. Bald (Cambridge: Cambridge University Press, 1929).

[20] Quoted from the edition by Gary Taylor in *Thomas Middleton: The Collected Works* (Oxford: Oxford University Press, 2010). The passage is only in a later version of the play.

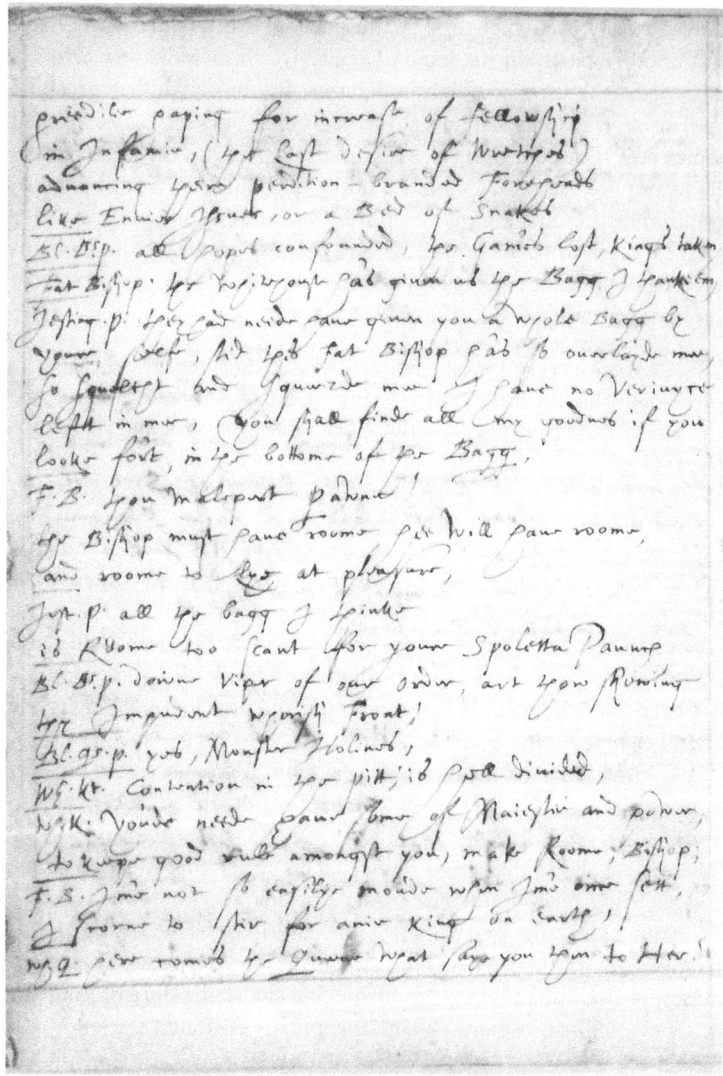

FIGURE 2.1 Thomas Middleton, *A Game at Chesse*, fol. 53ʳ Bridgewater manuscript, EL34 B17, The Huntington Library, San Marino, CA.

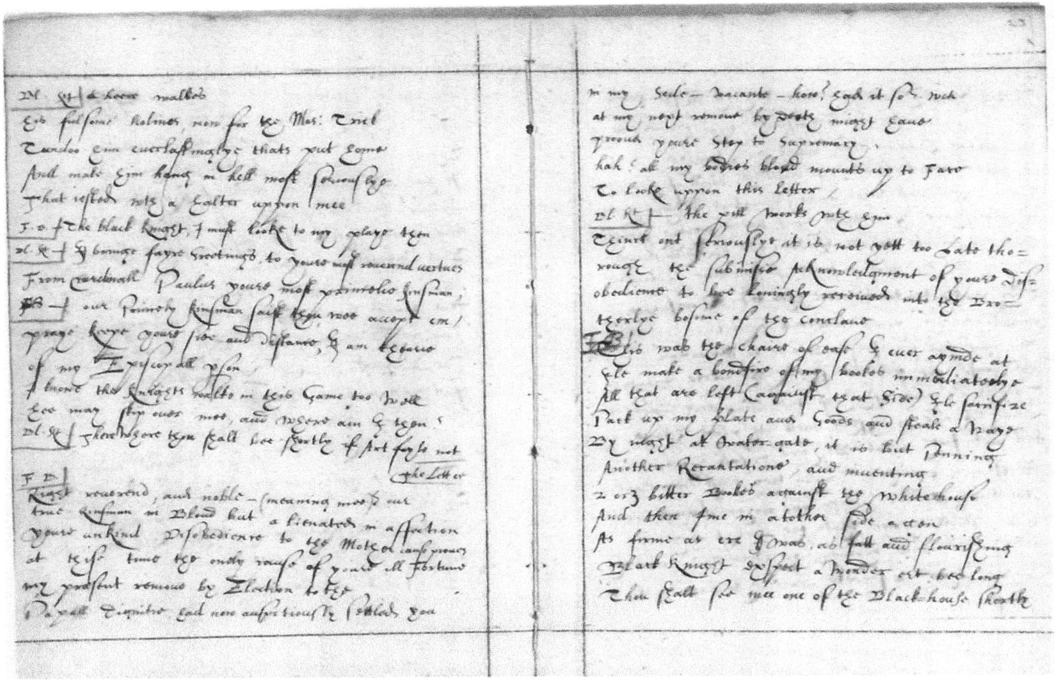

FIGURE 2.2 Thomas Middleton, A Game at Chesse, The Letter (3.1.33ff.), fols. 22ᵛ–23ʳ, Bridgewater manuscript, EL34 B17, The Huntington Library, San Marino, CA.

therefore (unlike the speech we have just considered) would be assumed to be prose. As in a number of instances in Crane's dramatic transcriptions, we see here one normal way of presenting prose in dialogue: the right-hand margin is not justified, and the shape of the text is determined not by metrics, but by how the scribe conceives the look of his page. In dramatic manuscripts of the period the distinction between verse and prose is a matter for the performer or reader to decide—the format often gives no guidance.

To realize that this is not verse one would have to be sensitive to the prosody; but confusion on the question would have been largely immaterial to anyone except a compositor, who had to translate the manuscript into the quite different conventions of printing: from the beginning of English printing with Caxton onward, lines of verse were capitalized and only the left hand margin was justified; whereas for prose, capitals marked the beginning of sentences, not of lines, and both margins were justified. Indeed, how difficult it was to establish the distinction between prose and verse in such cases is clear from the early printed editions of *A Game at Chesse*, which would have been set up from just this sort of copy. Figure 2.3 shows examples from two early quartos.

In the first example, the compositor realizes he is setting prose, and puts the letter in italics with a justified right margin, thereby distinguishing it from the verse dialogue, but misses the fact that the letter continues beyond the Black Knight's aside, and prints the last few lines as verse, and in roman—as dialogue, that is. In the second example, the compositor understands where the letter begins and ends, and puts the whole properly in italics, but misunderstands his copy to the extent of setting it as verse.

All this suggests that the question of verse versus prose was less pressing to Jacobean playwrights and to those concerned with the transmission of their texts than it has been to the subsequent editorial tradition. It was, for purely practical reasons, of most immediate concern to the typographer. Many speeches could be either; no character's nobility was impugned if he was detected speaking prose, nor was the dramatist's excellence vitiated if he was found to have written it. And if *The Tempest* had come down to us as a play by Middleton, we would have good evidence that the grounds for deciding whether Caliban's and Stephano's lines are really verse or prose are very shaky.

B. Kt. There where thou shalt be
Shortly, if arte faile not.

The Letter.

Right Reuerered and noble (meaning me) our true kinsman in affection, but alienated in blood, your vnkind disobedience to the mother cause, prooues the onely cause of your ill fortune at this time: My present remooue by generall election to the Papall dignity, had now auspiciously setled you in my Sede vacante (how had it so) which at my next remoous, by death might proued, your step to supremacy.
(Hah, all my bodies blood mounts to my face,
To looke vpon this letter.)

B. Kt. The pill workes with him,
Thinke on't seriously it is not yet too late then,
Through the submisse acknowledgment
Of your disobedience,
To be brotherly receiued into the louing
Bosome of the Conclaue.

Bl. Kni. There where thou shalt be shortly : if Art faile not.
Hee reades the Letter.

Fat B. Right reuerend and noble (meaning me) *Our Kins-man in blood, but alienated in affection; your Vnkinde disobedience to the Mother-cause, proues At this time the onely cause of your ill fortune: My present remooue by generall Election, to the Papall dignitie, had now auspiciously settled you In my Sede vacante* (how? had it so?) *which at my next remoue, By death, might haue proued your Step to Supremacie.*
Hah! all my Bodies blood mounts to my face
To looke vpon this letter.
Bl. Kni. The Pill workes with him.
Fat Bish. Thinke on't seriously, it is not yet too late Through the submisse acknowledgement of your Disobedience, to be louingly receaued into the Brotherly Bosome of the Conclaue.

FIGURE 2.3 The Letter, from two quartos of *A Game at Chesse*, STC (2nd edn) 17,882, fol. E4ʳ; and STC (2nd edn) 17,884, fol. E2ʳ.

Even when we are convinced that we know what the prosody of a passage is, and that the compositor has got it wrong, it is often difficult to conceive what he can have been responding to in his manuscript. Thus in both the first and second quartos of *Romeo and Juliet* (1597 and 1599), the Nurse's long account of the earthquake and the infant Juliet in 1.3, which reads as quite regular blank verse, is set not only as prose but in italics. Q2, which is a much fuller text, was at this point being set from Q1,[21] and therefore follows it; italics are used for the Nurse's speeches throughout this scene, and for a servant's lines at the end of the scene, but not thereafter in either text. G. I. Duthie suggests that for the Nurse's speech the compositor's copy was a fragment of the actor's part, and that that was written in an italic script, whereas for the rest of the play he had both Q1 and a manuscript written in an English hand—Duthie explains the italics of the Servant's lines as simply an aesthetic decision of the compositor. The speculation about the Nurse's part would be more persuasive if her part in other scenes were set in italics, but elsewhere in both quartos the only other things in italics are proper names, and the list of invitees to the Capulets' ball, which is labeled a letter and printed as prose. (It can, with a little adjustment, be construed as verse, and that is how it appears in all modern editions.)

If Duthie's speculation about the Nurse's speech is correct, it is significant that the passage is presented as prose—would the parts provided to the actors not have been lineated as verse? Perhaps not, and the issue of how to speak the passage was left up to the performer. However, in Q2 Mercutio's Queen Mab speech in 1.4 is also printed as prose up to line 91, the end of the page, but then concludes on the next page as verse. In this case, presumably the whole was verse in the manuscript but the typographer was pressed for space. The speech is set as verse throughout in Q1, but the manuscript from which the two editions were set cannot have been the same, since there are small but significant verbal differences in the two texts.

---

[21] Q1 was the source for Q2 from 1.2.57 to 1.3.36. See G. I. Duthie, "The Text of Shakespeare's *Romeo and Juliet*," *Studies in Bibliography*, 4 (1951/1952), 3–29.

Manners

Some editorial decisions are dictated by notions of linguistic propriety; and since these change from era to era, so does how we want Shakespearean characters to speak. Consider the history of a tiny crux in *The Winter's Tale*. When the courtier Camillo tries to argue King Leontes out of his jealousy of his wife Hermione's friendship with Polixenes, the visiting king of Bohemia, he says, in the folio:

> I cannot
> Beleeve this Crack to be in my dread Mistresse
> (So sovereignly being Honorable.)
> I have lov'd thee,

—and Leontes, in a fury, interrupts him with

> Make that thy question, and goe rot:
>
> (1.2.321–3)

This has occasioned much debate. Lewis Theobald, in his *Shakespeare Restored* (1726), essentially an attack on the recent Shakespeare edition of Alexander Pope, objected that Camillo could not call his sovereign "thee" (rather than "your majesty" or even "you," more dignified and formal) and gave the line to Leontes. Samuel Johnson concurred in the alteration, as did William Warburton. Most subsequent editors down to the present day have agreed that the pronoun is a problem, though since the eighteenth century the line has generally not been reassigned. The early twentieth-century editor John Dover Wilson found the issue significant enough to resolve it with an emendation: "T'have loved the—"; and Leontes's interruption thus prevents Camillo from naming the king of Bohemia. Ingenious as this is, it proved unpersuasive, and now looks preposterous; and editors continue to worry the question.

But why is it assumed that Camillo cannot call Leontes "thee"? Paulina calls him "thee," and much worse, in 3.2; the notion that Leontes cannot be addressed in this way depends on anachronistic attitudes towards both etiquette and kingship. The question of how to address the king was in fact quite an open one in the period: James I complained constantly that he was not treated with enough respect, and one of the major innovations of Charles I was the reform and codification of court protocol. But in a larger sense, the debate depends on an assumption that the court of legendary Sicilia is a literal reflection of actual court practice; and here it is sufficient to observe that if James I had decided to have his daughter Elizabeth exposed in infancy, he would not have been permitted to do so.

There is, no doubt, no way of preventing ourselves from seeing Shakespeare in our own image. Even the most radically historicized Shakespeares depend on a history that is constructed, and that will change with every generation. Stephen Greenblatt's Shakespeare in the best-selling *Will in the World*, richly informed as it is by Renaissance culture and politics, is obviously as much a creation of our own age as William Poel's "authentically Elizabethan" stage productions were of late Victorian England. Poel, an actor, producer, and theater manager, presented versions of plays by Shakespeare, Jonson, Marlowe, and others that he declared were recreations of Elizabethan stage practice. His texts, however, were those of the published editions, not of any versions that Elizabethan or Jacobean actors might have performed. These were uncut, and all that was authentic about them was that they were presented on an open stage with very little scenery. Moreover, Poel cast women, not boys, in the women's roles, and his attempt to stage the first quarto of *Hamlet* in 1881 met with such indignation that he substituted the familiar Q2 text, treating Q1 simply as a guide for cutting the play.

But the striking thing about the editorial practices I have been considering is that they do not show us revising Shakespeare's characters to act as we act. On the contrary, what is suppressed in them is precisely our deepest convictions about the constitution of our own psychology, our insistence on the pre-rational, irrational, libidinous, and unconscious sources of human behavior. This is what we do not want our Shakespeare to mirror. No one with any experience of fifteen-year-old girls believes that they are, like the Miranda of modern productions of *The Tempest*, obedient, passive, and non-sexual. Many critics have observed that Leontes's jealousy in *The Winter's Tale*, violent and unsubstantiated, is in fact realistic, far more true to human experience than Othello's super-rationalized passion, which has a villain for its agent and depends on a stolen handkerchief. To render Miranda an innocent and rationalize Leontes's jealousy (for example, by arguing that Hermione and Polixenes may have given the impression of intimacy, or presenting the action that way in performance) is not to make *The Tempest* and *The Winter's Tale* more true to life, but to distance and sentimentalize them.

Finally, to emend or argue away the directness of Camillo's address to his sovereign, to assume that the relation of subject to ruler is necessarily one of circumspection and concessiveness, is to rewrite the nature of authority and the question of what is owed to it, arguably the central issue in *The Winter's Tale*—as it has been a central issue for our own time. And perhaps this is the real point: the editorial process has worked not to keep Shakespeare our contemporary, but to deflect Shakespearean drama from our deepest concerns.

| 3 |

From Stage to Page

How do we know what the relation was between whatever texts have come down to us and what playgoers saw in Shakespeare's theater? Since our claims about the effects of Shakespearean drama are necessarily based on the printed texts, it would seem essential to consider this question, and not simply to assume that we can read backward from the latter to the former. As Paul Menzer observes, "our thinking about backstage scripts tends to be guided by printed texts, which turns manuscriptural mess into typographical uniformity as we back-project print form onto handwritten documents."[1] I do not, of course, pretend that we are in any position to supply an answer; but I also think the question is a larger one than we have made it, and it is necessary to understand its full implications before we try to move beyond it. Obviously readings are performances too, especially readings aloud, as they typically were until the last century. But reading performances are inflected by the decisions made by the editor and printer of the book. In texts like *Tamburlaine* or *The Spanish Tragedy*, which acknowledge that they have been rewritten to be printed, the reader is not performing the same play that Marlowe's or Kyd's audiences saw. All printed texts, including Shakespeare's, have gone through some editorial process.

---

[1] Paul Menzer, *The* Hamlets (Newark, DE: University of Delaware Press, 2008), p. 29.

Simon Forman

I begin with two well-known pieces of evidence, the astrologer and physician Simon Forman's accounts of *Macbeth* and *The Winter's Tale*, both of which he saw at the Globe in the spring of 1611 and described in his journal. These have been examined often, and found tantalizingly, maddeningly unforthcoming. Both give significantly different versions of the plays from those we know, omitting some things we would call essential, including others that are not part of our texts and that look to us irrelevant or even impossible, and which have no known source outside the play and defy any simple explanation. Nevertheless, in some very basic respects Forman's accounts share assumptions with modern critical and editorial practice.

Forman's version of *Macbeth* opens not with the witches and the report of the battle, but with this:

> Macbeth and Banquo, 2 noblemen of Scotland, riding through a wood, there stood before them 3 women fairies or nymphs, and saluted Macbeth, saying 3 times unto him, "Hail Macbeth, king of Codon, for thou shall be a king but shall beget no kings," etc.[2]

Forman then records the prophecy that Banquo will beget kings. When Macbeth and Banquo arrive at Duncan's court, Forman says that Macbeth is made "forthwith Prince of Northumberland" (at this point in the folio text it is *Malcolm* who is dubbed Prince of *Cumberland*, "a step," Macbeth says, "On which I must fall down, or else o'erleap, | For in my way it lies" [1.5.48–9]). There follows in Forman's account a very powerful scene that also does not exist in our play:

> And when Macbeth had murdered the king, the blood on his hands could not be washed off by any means, nor from his wife's hands which handled the bloody daggers in hiding them. By which means they became both much amazed and affronted.

---

[2] My text is from the modernized version provided by the Folger Library. The journal is in the Bodleian Library (MS Ashmole 208), headed *The Bocke of Plaies and Notes therof per Forman for Common Pollicie*. It is reproduced online, with both diplomatic and modernized transcriptions, at https://shakespearedocumented.folger.edu/resource/document/formans-account-seeing-plays-globe-macbeth-cymbeline-winters-tale, accessed January 14, 2023. This section begins at fol. 200; the account of *Macbeth* begins at fol. 207r.

There is no mention in Forman's *Macbeth* of the apparition scene, or of the prophecies relating to Birnam Wood and the man not born of woman, or of the moving forest, though Forman does record, as an afterthought, Lady Macbeth's sleepwalking scene.

The Winter's Tale as Forman describes it is much closer to our play. His notes are, with one exception, a reasonably accurate summary of the play as we know it.[3] The exception, however, is a huge one: Forman either fails to mention or did not see Hermione's resurrection, the statue coming to life.

Some of these discrepancies have been accounted for by assuming that Forman consulted Shakespeare's sources. Macbeth and Banquo cannot have been "riding through a wood" on the stage of the Globe, but a woodcut in Holinshed depicts them meeting the witches on horseback (see figure 3.1), and reference to Holinshed would also account for Forman's characterization of the women as "fairies or nymphes": in the *Chronicles* they are "Nimphes or Feiries."

FIGURE 3.1   Macbeth and Banquo meet the "Nimphes or Feiries." Raphaell Holinshed, *The Firste Volume of the Chronicles of England, Scotlande and Ireland* (1577), "The Historie of Scotlande," p. 243.

---

[3] A digitized facsimile with both diplomatic and modernized transcriptions are at the website cited above; the account of *The Winter's Tale* begins on fol. 201v.

But the source in this case also raises new problems, because if we assume that Forman checked Holinshed to refresh his memory of the play, how can we explain his version of Macbeth's title Thane of Cawdor as "king of Codon"—Codon looks like an *auditory* error for Cawdor (Holinshed spells the name Cawder)—and how can we explain the creation of Macbeth as Prince of Northumberland, where Holinshed, like the folio, has Malcolm created Prince of Cumberland? And of course there is no known source for Forman's scene of Macbeth and Lady Macbeth "much amazed and affronted" at their inability to wash Duncan's blood off their hands.

Did Forman's lively imagination simply add this scene to his recollection of the play? The answer here may very well be yes: Forman would then be conflating Macbeth's "multitudinous seas incarnadine" speech with Lady Macbeth's desperate handwashing pantomime in the sleepwalking scene, to produce the kind of clear moral emblem he found attractive. Certainly it is difficult to imagine Lady Macbeth speaking lines like "What's done is done" and "This is the very painting of your fear" after such a scene as Forman describes. In fact, we *must* argue Forman's evidence away unless we are prepared to conclude that the King's Men in 1611 were presenting a radically different *Macbeth* from the one that has survived—a possibility, certainly, but one that few editors will care to entertain, and which would certainly not be possible to take into account editorially. Forman's scene, of course, need not be entirely imaginary. He may be memorializing a particularly effective piece of stage business when the Macbeth of 1611 asked "Will all great Neptune's ocean wash this blood | Clean from my hand?"

As for the absence from Forman's *Winter's Tale* of Hermione's statue, it is also absent from the story in Robert Greene's *Pandosto*, Shakespeare's source; but did Forman simply substitute the source for the play? This is harder to argue away than the handwashing scene in *Macbeth*. The statue scene has been, for almost three centuries, not only the emotional culmination of the drama, but an absolutely essential element of the plot. It is difficult for us to imagine a spectator either failing to recall it or thinking it not worth mentioning. Here we inevitably take refuge in *ad hominem* arguments: Forman is our only witness, hardly a reliable one, and we would surely be overstepping the bounds of his very shifty evidence if we used it to assert that there was a version of the play in

1611 that did not include the restoration of Hermione.[4] The most we can assert—it is in fact a great deal—is that this contemporary spectator preserved for himself a version of *The Winter's Tale* quite different from one that we believe any of us would have taken away from a performance of the play. It is perhaps relevant that of the twenty seventeenth-century allusions to the play recorded in *The Shakespere Allusion Book*, not one refers to the statue scene.[5]

What more can we say of these, the only eyewitness accounts we possess of two of Shakespeare's most perennially compelling plays in Shakespeare's own theater? We assume the accounts cannot be correct because they are contradicted by the surviving texts. We declare them unreliable because they are influenced (or "contaminated") by other works, some of which (e.g., the sources) we think we can identify, but most of which we cannot even begin to imagine. I am not arguing that we are wrong to deal with Forman in this way, but the problems we face with his versions of Shakespeare are at most somewhat exaggerated instances of the problems we face with all versions of Shakespeare, from bad and good quartos and the folio on down through the whole history of editorial and critical practice. And our appeal to the texts as the bottom line is far more problematic than, historically, we have been willing to allow.

The problem is precisely the texts: What are our texts? It hardly needs to be insisted that none of our texts is original, that every work we possess by Shakespeare has been through some editorial process. And even if a Shakespeare manuscript were discovered tomorrow, if we suddenly found those magical foul papers (the author's rough drafts, as opposed

---

[4] As an editorial argument, however, this is not inconceivable, and the combination of Forman plus a source has been used to argue both for and against emendation. Stanley Wells and Gary Taylor, in their edition of *Cymbeline* in the Oxford Shakespeare, emend the name Imogen to Innogen, noting that the name is so given both in Forman's account of the play and in Holinshed, and that Shakespeare elsewhere—once, for a ghost character in *Much Ado*—uses the name Innogen. It would, of course, be as reasonable to argue that the unique, ghostly Innogen is the erroneous form, that Forman got his version of the name from Holinshed, and that Shakespeare was not controlled by his sources in this matter, any more than he was in numerous others.

[5] With the possible exception of Dryden, who in 1672 suggested that *The Winter's Tale* was one of a group of Shakespeare plays "grounded upon impossibilities," perhaps referring to the statue. See C. M. Ingleby et al., *The Shakespere Allusion Book* (new edition, London: Oxford University Press, 1932), p. 2.175.

to "fair copies") to whose elusive authority all editorial claims are ultimately referred, it would not simply solve all our problems. We would have to edit it before we could draw conclusions about it, and the editorial process would involve all the familiar decisions about what was really intended or meant, and these would inevitably be based on the editor's own assumptions about what the text ought to look like, and different editors would produce different texts. The conclusions, that is, really come first, not last; and whatever Shakespeare's foul papers reveal to us will inevitably be perceived through the distorting glass of our own assumptions. This is the respect in which Simon Forman is a model for the editor and critic; it is a mistake to believe that our sense of Shakespeare, whether we are scientific bibliographers or casual playgoers, is not "contaminated" by a myriad of other texts and experiences. Indeed, Shakespeare's own working conditions, the requirements of his playhouse and the fact that his texts were to be spoken by actors, might be considered, as Humphrey Moseley considered them, a form of contamination; hence the modern critical desire to see Shakespeare as always really writing for publication, an audience of readers.

Romeo and Juliet

In an essay called "Two Household Friends," I considered the case of the two quartos of *Romeo and Juliet*, neither of which can have been the text of the play on the stage, but which are interestingly interdependent, and which allow us to see something about the process of translation of a play into a book in action.[6] For a long time the differences between Q1 and Q2, and the presumed defectiveness of Q1, were explained by invoking the concept of memorial reconstruction: Q1 was claimed to be a text put together by actors with deficient memories. But over the years the arguments postulating memorial reconstruction in Q1 looked increasingly tenuous; and they have now been effectively demolished by Paul Werstine and Lukas Erne, though both retain them to account for small

---

[6] The essay appears in my collection *The Invention of Shakespeare and Other Essays* (Philadelphia: University of Pennsylvania Press, 2022), pp. 65–82.

individual moments.⁷ But memorial reconstruction will not help with any of the problems I consider. Here is Erne's concluding summary of his argument about the relation of the two texts, which seems to me the best proposal, an elegant account of a very complex situation: "Shakespeare's original script as reflected by Q2 seems likely to have been abridged before the play reached the stage, but this abridgment accounts only for a portion of the divengences between Q1 and Q2, the omissions, but not the textual differences. While the latter seem partly a matter of memorial agency, it seems possible that small-scale authorial revision also contributed a share towards them."⁸ I quote this first, because, as will become clear, it seems to me in general right; but there are some interesting cases that it does not account for. My essay was not framed as a debate with Erne, but as an examination of some puzzles that Erne's edition got me thinking about. Needless to say, I concluded that the situation is even more complicated than his complicated formulation allows.

Consider the Prologue, famously a sonnet—but only in Q2; in Q1 it appears as two quatrains and two couplets. Now: If Q2 is the prior text, and Q1 is a revised version for the stage, did the reviser not realize that the Prologue was a sonnet? If the reviser was Shakespeare, was there some reason for changing it and making it *not* a sonnet? Or is this, right at the outset, a bit of memorial reconstruction, with the reporter forgetting the first and third lines of a quatrain? All these explanations are obviously dubious; and it seems much more likely that the revision went the other way, that Q1 at this point was the prior text, and the Prologue did not start out as a sonnet, but turning it into a sonnet was a bright second idea. Is there a point to its being a sonnet (or becoming one)? Sonnets do figure significantly elsewhere in the play, forming part of the action during the ball scene, where the lovers' dialogue is an extended sonnet, with an extra quatrain after the couplet—the first

---

⁷ Paul Werstine, "A Century of 'Bad' Shakespeare Quartos," *Shakespeare Quarterly*, 50.3 (1999), 310–33, esp. 326–7 and 332–3; Lukas Erne, ed. *The First Quarto of Romeo and Juliet* (Cambridge: Cambridge University Press, 2007). I am also indebted to Jonathan Goldberg's thrilling demolition of spurious bibliographical arguments in "'What? in a names that which we call a Rose,' The Desired Texts of *Romeo and Juliet*," in *Crisis in Editing: Texts of the English Renaissance*, ed. Randall McLeod (New York: AMS Press, 1994), pp. 173–202.

⁸ Erne, *First Quarto*, p. 24.

expression of their love is a sonnet, though the sonnet cannot quite contain what they have to say. (Bradin Cormack has ingeniously suggested that the extra quatrain is the beginning of a second sonnet, interrupted by the Nurse.)[9] That might suggest that making the Prologue a sonnet, introducing the love story with a sonnet, was an afterthought—perhaps considered ultimately a mistake, since it seems not to have remained in the text: the folio omits the Prologue entirely.

In both quartos the Prologue is printed in italics, but whereas Q2's Prologue is clearly part of the action, supplied with a speaker identified as a *Chorus*, Q1's Prologue is printed to look like a prefatory poem. So, if Q1 is, as Erne puts it, as close as we can come to the play on Shakespeare's stage, the typography of Q1 at this point is treating the play as a book. The two, moreover, prepare us for rather different plays. Q2 gives us the version that has become standard:

> *Two housholds both alike in dignitie,*
> *(In faire* Verona *where we lay our Scene)*
> *From aunctient grudge, breake to new mutinie,*
> *Where civill bloud makes civill hands uncleane:*[10]

To begin with, the dignity and the symmetry of the two families is stressed—they are "both alike"—and this initially seems to be an aspect of "fair Verona," one of the things that make the city decorous and beautiful. But then the dignity turns out to involve an ancient grudge, which eventuates in "new mutiny"—a developing process is implied, and line 4 describes a continuing state of civil war. "Civil," like "dignity," has unexpected double senses: "civil blood" could mean "natural courtesy," an aspect of the dignity that makes the city fair; but by the end of the line we see that it means just the opposite, "civic warfare." In line 5, the "loins" that give life to their children are "fatal," both death-dealing and ominous or fated, and the lovers are "star-crossed," doomed by the malignancy of their horoscopes. This bears on the question of where the ultimate responsibility for the tragedy lies—if the lovers are star-crossed, then the feuding families with their ancient grudge are star-crossed too: they are genetically star-crossed. However badly the

---

[9] "Shakespeare's Narcissus, Sonnet's Echo," in *The Forms of Renaissance Thought*, ed. Leonard Barkan, Bradin Cormack, and Sean Keilen (Houndsmill: Palgrave Macmillan, 2009), p. 130.

[10] Quotations from the two quartos are normalized transcriptions of the original texts, 1597 and 1599.

families behave in what is obviously a continuing tragedy, fate, the stars, their horoscopes are responsible. The lovers are "misadventured, piteous," and their love in line 9 has a "fearful passage": they have bad luck, and we are to pity and fear for them—this is an Aristotelian view of the nature of tragedy as the Renaissance understood Aristotle: misadventure in the plot, pity and terror in the response, but no hamarteia, no hero with a tragic flaw.

The play promised by the Prologue of Q1 is significantly different, so different that editors have more than once declared it nonsense:

> TWo houshold Frends alike in dignitie,
> (In faire Verona, where we lay our Scene)
> From civill broyles broke into enmitie,
> Whose civill warre makes civill hands uncleane.

Is "household friends" even possible? What then would "civil broils" mean? Courteous disagreements that break into open warfare? Possible—maybe even nice: this gives us a progression, and no ancient grudge—it does look as if Q2 is a revision. The ancient grudge is referred to later in both versions of the play, but in Q2's preliminary summary it dominates and determines the action. In Q1 the households are friends; they move from "civil broils" to uncivil ones. Perhaps most significantly, it is only Q2 that anticipates the end of the civil strife through the lovers' death, promising an ethically satisfying conclusion. Was that really cut from Q1, not added to Q2?

What are we to make of the sudden move into the theatrical present in both texts, the reference to the two-hour traffic of our stage? This is the only Shakespeare play that calls attention to the length of time its action is to occupy in the theater (*The Tempest* does note that its action is taking place in real time, though the amount of real time is unclear). But Q1 can be performed in two hours, whereas Q2 would take more like three. Does Q2 begin by artificially speeding up its action, making us expect a shorter play; or is Q2 a draft that expects to be cut by an hour in the process of being prepared for the stage? Is two hours even intended as a real estimate of the play's timing, or is it simply a way of saying how the time will seem to fly?[11]

---

[11] Tiffany Stern, in a fascinating article on systems of time-measurement in the early modern period, argues that "two hours" is not to be taken literally, and cites instances of plays being said to take three hours, or even more. The measurement of time was,

There is a second chorus-sonnet in Q2, and it constitutes one of the most baffling elements of the text. In Q2, the second chorus looks like part of an uninterrupted action. It comes at the beginning of what is in modern editions Act 2 (neither the quarto nor folio texts have act and scene divisions), and implies a passage of time and a series of secret meetings and stolen kisses between the first two acts—between, that is, the ball scene and the balcony scene. These two scenes, however, clearly proceed without pause: Romeo leaves the ball, eludes his companions, and climbs into Juliet's garden, where she is, on her balcony, for the first time, sighing her heart out for him. Nor can the second chorus be projecting future action; Act 2 is also continuous—the whole point is how fast it all goes, "too rash, too unadvised, too sudden," no time for secret meetings now or later. This chorus is impossible in the play as we have it. It suggests an earlier version of the play more directly based on its source in Arthur Brooke's *Romeus and Juliet*, in which the wooing does cover several months—it may be relevant that the prologue to Brooke's long poem is also a sonnet. The second chorus is almost invariably omitted in performance, since it contradicts the action. It has no parallel in Q1, though it is, oddly, retained in the folio text. Does its presence in Q2 and F merely indicate the desire for another sonnet? It does remind us, in any case, that the texts of plays are not the plays, and that reading a book is different from going to theater.

Establishing priority between Q1 and Q2, then, is not a straightforward matter. Q2 retains bits of what must be a plan for the play that was subsequently abandoned, but also includes bits that look like sophistications and fine-tunings of Q1—there are others throughout the play. Q1 in turn in many places is clearly an edited or cut version of the text in Q2. Each of the texts is in some respects prior to the other. Complicating the situation is the fact that the manuscript behind Q2 was apparently defective in scenes 2 and 3, for which Q1 was used as the copy text. We do not at all know, however, that the problems with the manuscript were limited to this section, and additions, adjustments, or revisions may have been required (or simply felt to be desirable) elsewhere as well. This script is being turned into a book; there is no reason, moreover, to assume that the reviser was Shakespeare.

---

moreover, very approximate. "Time for Shakespeare: Hourglasses, Sundials, Clocks, and Early Modern Theatre," *Journal of the British Academy*, 3 (2015), 1–33.

4

The Example of *Macbeth*

The only text of *Macbeth* surviving from Shakespeare's time is the one in the folio, which is demonstrably a revision. It includes songs for the witches in act 3, scene 5, given in the text only as incipits ("Come away, come away, etc." "Black spirits, etc."). These are songs from Middleton's play *The Witch*. In performance they would have been accompanied by dances, which means that in the theater these scenes took a good deal longer than they do on the page, especially since the text does not include the whole of the songs, but only their first few words. The manuscript of Sir William Davenant's version of *Macbeth*, prepared around 1664, includes the whole text of the witches' songs from Middleton—these are really musical dialogues, short scenes. The fact that Davenant did not supply his own witches' material at these points, as he did elsewhere, suggests that the Middleton material was already a standard feature of the play: *The Witch* was not printed till the late eighteenth century, but Davenant had access to the King's Men's papers. I have assumed in my Pelican edition of *Macbeth* that the inclusion of all the Middleton material dates from the revision printed in the folio, and I therefore included the complete text of the songs.

The elaboration of the witches' roles could have taken place anywhere up to about fifteen years after the play was first performed, but the presence of the Middleton material suggests that Shakespeare was no longer available to do the revising, which presumes a date after 1614. It is an unusual text in other ways, too, clearly not, or not entirely, printed from a promptbook. Why, only a decade after the play was written, would augmenting the witches' roles have seemed a good idea? To begin with, by 1610 or so witchcraft, magic, and the diabolical were good theater business—Barnabe Barnes's *The Devil's Charter* was at the Globe in the same season as *Macbeth*, and John Marston's *The Wonder of Women*, which includes sorcery scenes, was at the Blackfriars: rival companies mounted competing plays when something was especially popular—*The Merchant of Venice* coincides with a revival of Marlowe's *The Jew of Malta*; *Hamlet*, Marston's *The Malcontent*, and the revived and revised *Spanish Tragedy* were all being performed in 1601, *Henry IV* was competing with *Sir John Oldcastle*, a play that undertakes to correct Shakespeare's version of Falstaff. Jonson's *Masque of Queens*, performed at court in 1609, inaugurated a decade of sorcery plays and masques, including *The Tempest*, Ford, Dekker, and Rowley's *The Witch of Edmonton*, Jonson's *The Alchemist* and *The Devil is an Ass*, and the revived and rewritten *Doctor Faustus*.

The ubiquitousness of theatrical magic is reason enough for the elaboration of the witches in *Macbeth*, but it does not account for everything. When Macbeth, after the murder of Banquo, goes to consult the witches, and they show him a terrifying vision of Banquo's heirs, Hecate proposes a little entertainment to cheer him up:

> I'll charm the air to give a sound
> While you perform your antic round,
> That this great king may kindly say
> Our duties did his welcome pay.
> (4.1.145–8)

The tone of the scene here changes significantly: the witches are not professional and peremptory any more, they are lighthearted, gracious, and deferential. We may choose to treat this as a moment of heavy irony, though Macbeth does not seem to respond to it as such; but if it is not ironic, the change of tone suggests that the "great king" addressed in this passage is not the king on stage, but instead a real king in the audience, Banquo's descendant and the king of both Scotland and England.

The editors of both the recent Oxford and Cambridge editions have resisted the suggestion that this moment in *Macbeth* reflects the local conditions of a court performance, observing that nothing in the scene positively requires such an assumption. Richard Dutton, in his very persuasive book *Shakespeare, Court Dramatist*, however, noting that performances at court were typically much longer than those at the public theaters (and therefore that the unusual length of a number of Shakespeare plays indicates adaptations for the court), proposes that the shortness of both *Macbeth* and *The Tempest* indicates subsequent adaptations for the Blackfriars, which required shorter plays because performances there included a good deal of music.[1] (Of course, with the full Hecate scenes that are not included in the folio text, the play would have been a good deal longer.)[2] If Dutton is correct, however, it would have been the text of the court production of *Macbeth* that had become standard and was the version that was adapted to the needs of the Blackfriars.

Although there is no record of a court performance, King James surely must have wanted to see a play that included both witches and his ancestors. What are the implications if we assume that the text we have derives from a revision to take into account the presence of the king, and that his interest in witchcraft also accounts for the augmentation of the witches' scenes, so that the "filthy, black and midnight hags" became graciously entertaining after they finished being ominously informative? Such a play would be significantly less author-centered than our familiar text: First because it is reviser-centered—and the presence of the Middleton scenes implies that Shakespeare was not the reviser—and second, because it is patron-centered, taking a particular audience into account. To this extent Shakespeare's *Macbeth* is already, in the folio version, a significantly collaborative enterprise. But if this is correct, it also means that this version of *Macbeth* is a special case, devised for a single occasion, a performance at court, which was then re-adapted to the needs of the play in repertory, the play for the public.[3]

---

[1] Richard Dutton, *Shakespeare, Court Dramatist* (Oxford: Oxford University Press, 2016), pp. 37, 281.

[2] As it is in both Gary Taylor's edition in the Oxford Middleton and in my Pelican Shakespeare, both of which include the Middleton additions.

[3] Dutton sees a similar process of adaptation in *The Tempest*, arguing that the masque in act 4 makes much better sense as a celebration of the marriage of Princess Elizabeth and the Elector Palatine (we know the play was performed at court as part of their wedding festivities) than as an celebration of the betrothal of Miranda and Ferdinand. I find this claim unpersuasive: there were fourteen plays presented at court before the royal couple, including *Othello* and *The Maid's Tragedy*, not (one hopes) chosen for any particular relevance to this marriage. At the same time, there is good evidence that *The Tempest* was a Blackfriars play.

This leads to another question: How did this text become the standard version; why was it the right version to include in the folio? It needs to be emphasized that this is a question whether we assume that a performance before the king is involved or not: there is no denying that this is a revised text with non-Shakespearean material. Most attempts to deal with this issue beg the question, assuming that what we have is indeed the wrong text, and that Shakespeare's first editors would never have included it if they had had any alternative. The right text, the text we want (the promptbook, or even better, Shakespeare's holograph) must have been unavailable, lost—burned, perhaps, in the destruction of the Globe in 1613, as if only a conflagration could explain the refusal of Heminges and Condell (who promise, after all, the true original copies) to give us what we want. But perhaps it was included precisely because it was the right text, whether because by 1620 this, quite simply, was the play, or, more interestingly, because the best version of the play was the one prepared for the king.

This would make it an apparent anomaly in the folio, a version of the play designed for a single, special occasion, rather than the standard public theater version. In fact, the play as it stands in the folio is anomalous in a number of respects. It is a very unusual play textually: it is very short, the shortest of the tragedies (half the length of *Hamlet*, a third shorter than the average), shorter, too than all the comedies except *The Comedy of Errors*. It looks, moreover, as if the version we have has not only been augmented with material for the witches, but has also been cut and rearranged, producing some real muddles in the narrative: for example, the scene between Lenox and the Lord (3.6), reporting Macduff's defection to England, action that has not happened yet; or the notorious syntactic puzzles of the account of the battle in the opening scenes; or the confusion of the final battle, in which Macbeth is slain by Macduff onstage, and twenty lines later Macduff re-enters with his head.

Revision and cutting were, of course, standard and necessary procedures in a theater where the normal playing time was two or three hours; but if theatrical cuts are to explain the peculiarities of this text, why was it cut so peculiarly, not to say ineptly? Arguments that make the muddles not the result of cutting but an experiment in surreal and expressionistic dramaturgy only produce more questions, rendering the play a total anomaly, both in Shakespeare's work and in the drama of the period. The very presence of the witches is unusual. Shakespeare makes use of the supernatural from time to time—ghosts in *Richard III*, *Julius Caesar*, and most notably here and in *Hamlet* (but why a ghost for Banquo but not Duncan?), fairies and their magic in *A Midsummer Night's Dream*, the spirits and Prospero's sorcery in *The Tempest*, Joan of Arc's and Marjory Jourdain's in the *Henry VI* plays, and Rosalind's claim to be a magician at the end of *As You Like It*—but there is no other play in which witches and witchcraft are such an integral element of the plot.

The Witches

Indeed, whether or not King James was in the audience, the fact that it is the witches who provide the royal entertainment can hardly be accidental. The king, the company's patron, was intensely interested in witchcraft; his dialogue on the subject, *Dæmonologie*, first published in Edinburgh in 1597, was reissued three times upon his accession to the English throne in 1603. This and the *Basilicon Doron*, his philosophy of kingship, were the two works that he chose to introduce himself to his English subjects, and witchcraft and kingship have an intimate relationship in the Jacobean royal ideology. This is a culture in which the supernatural and witchcraft, even for sceptics, are as much part of reality as religious truth is. Like the ghost in *Hamlet*, the reality of the witches in *Macbeth* is not in question; the question, as in *Hamlet*, is why they are present and how far to believe them.

Like the ghost, too, the witches are quintessential theatrical devices: they dance and sing, perform wonders, appear and disappear, fly, produce visions—do, in short, all the things that, historically, we have gone to the theater to see. They open the play and set the tone for it. On Shakespeare's stage they would simply have materialized through a trap door, but Shakespeare's audience believed in magic already. Our rationalistic theater requires something more theatrically elaborate, some serious mystification. For Shakespeare's audience, the mystification is built into their physical appearance, which defies categories: they look like men and are women. The indeterminacy of their gender is the first thing Banquo calls attention to. This is a defining element of their nature, a paradox that identifies them as witches: a specifically female propensity to evil—being a witch—is defined by its apparent masculinity. This is also, of course, one of the central charges leveled at Shakespeare's theater itself, the ambiguity of its gender roles, the fact that on Shakespeare's stage the women are really male. But the gender ambiguity relates as well to roles within the play: Lady Macbeth unsexes herself, and accuses her husband of being afraid to act like a man. What constitutes acting like a man in this play? The answer seems to be killing. Killing is the one thing Lady Macbeth says she cannot do:

> Had he not resembled
> My father as he slept, I had done't
>
> (2.2.12–13).

Unsexing herself renders her, unexpectedly, not a man but a child, and thus incapable of murder. Indeed, the definitive relation between murder and manhood applies to heroes as well as villains. When Macduff is told of the murder of his wife and children and is urged to "Dispute it like a man," he replies that he must first feel it as a man (4.3.221–3). Whatever this says about his sensitivity and family feeling, it also says that murder makes you feel like a man.

The unsettling quality of the witches goes beyond gender. Their language is paradoxical; fair is foul and foul is fair; when the battle's lost and won. One way of looking at this is to say that it constitutes no paradox at all: any battle that is lost has also been won, but by somebody else. The person who describes a battle as lost and won is either on both sides or on neither; what is fair for one side is bound to be foul for the other. In a brilliantly subversive essay, Harry Berger, Jr., suggested that the witches are in fact accurate spokespeople for the play, and are telling the truth about its world, that there really are no ethical standards in it, no right and wrong sides.[4] Duncan certainly starts out sounding like a good king: the rhetoric of his monarchy is full of claims about its sacredness, about the deference that is due to it, how it is part of a natural hierarchy descending from God, how the king is divinely anointed, and so forth. But in fact none of this is borne out by the play: Duncan's rule is utterly chaotic, and maintaining it depends on constant warfare—the battle that opens the play, after all, is not an invasion but a rebellion. Duncan's rule has never commanded the deference it

---

[4] "The Early Scenes of Macbeth: Preface to a New Interpretation," in his collection *Making Trifles of Terrors* (Stanford: Stanford University Press, 1997), pp. 70–97.

claims for itself; deference is not natural to it. In upsetting that sense of the deference Macbeth feels he owes to Duncan, the witches are releasing into the play something the play both overtly denies and implicitly articulates: that there is no basis whatever for the values asserted on Duncan's behalf; that the primary characteristic of his rule (perhaps of any rule in the world of the play) is not order but rebellion.

The Padua Folio

In the library of the University of Padua there is a Shakespeare first folio in which two plays, *Macbeth* and *Measure for Measure*, have been marked up for performance.[5] The book came to the university in the mid-seventeenth century, the gift of the British consul in the Veneto John Hobson, Sr., along with treatises on mathematics, navigation, and commerce, and Sir John Harington's translation of *Orlando Furioso*—a gentleman's library. The editing of the two marked-up plays has been dated to before 1640; they were prepared, according to G. Blakemore Evans, by a professional hand for a professional company.[6] About their actual use we can say nothing, but they allow us to see what a performing text of Shakespeare looked like within a couple of decades of the playwright's death.

---

[5] The beginning few lines of *The Winter's Tale* are also marked up. Facsimiles are in G. Blakemore Evans, ed., *Shakespearean Prompt-Books of the Seventeenth Century*, Vol. I: *The Padua "Macbeth"* (Charlottesville: University of Virginia Press, 1960); Vol. II, *The Padua "Measure for Measure"* (1963). The history of the volume is discussed by Lavinia Prosdocimi, "Un fondo appartenuto alla *natio Anglica*. Il *First Folio* e altri libri inglesi della Biblioteca universitaria," in Ester Pietrobon, ed., *Intellettuali e Uomini di Corte* (Roma: Donzelli Editore, 2021), pp. 205–16. There is also a promptbook of the two parts of *Henry the Fourth*, a scribal transcription based on the quartos, which dates from the early 1620s, before the publication of the folio. This was prepared for a private production at Sir Edward Dering's country estate—Dering was the first purchaser of record of the Shakespeare folio; he bought two copies in the week after publication. His *Henry IV* underwent far more radical revision than the two Padua plays, amalgamating the two parts and reducing their approximately 6,000 lines to roughly 3,500, but also including additional original material. It reveals a great deal about both the sophistication of amateur theater and the way a popular Shakespearean text was regarded in the early seventeenth century. See *The History of King Henry the Fourth as revised by Sir Edward Dering, Bart.*, ed. George Walton Williams and G. Blakemore Evans (Charlottesville: University of Virginia Press, 1974).

[6] *Padua "Macbeth,"* General Introduction, p. 10. Evans's dating has been amended by Lavinia Prosdocimi in the essay cited above.

The editing throughout is designed to speed up action and reduce dialogue, not to clarify or simplify.[7] A great deal of what is most characteristically Shakespearean—poetic imagery, metaphorical complexity—are cut, including what have become some of the most famous passages in the two plays. Here is Macbeth's "Tomorrow, and tomorrow, and tomorrow" speech as it appears in the promptbook:

> To morrow, and to morrow, and to morrow,
> Creepes in this petty pace from day to day,
> To the last Syllable of Recorded time:
> And all our yesterdayes, have lighted Fooles
> The way to dusty death. Out, out, breefe Candle,
> Life's but a walking Shadow. It is a Tale
> Told by an Ideot, full of sound and fury
> Signifying nothing.

What is for us the climax of the speech, the poor player who struts and frets his hour upon the stage and then is heard no more, which brings it home to Shakespeare, is deleted.

The cutting of *Measure for Measure* is more systematic. Long speeches are shortened, debates are tightened and simplified, and—especially—poetic complexity is removed. Much of the Duke's explanation to the Friar about why he left his throne is deleted. In Isabella's first interview with Angelo the arguments on both sides are effectively eviscerated; indeed, the omission from this version of the play of what were to become its most famous passages is notable. In all, the reviser cut 579 of the play's 2,660 lines, or about 22 percent, a larger proportion than the *Macbeth* cuts, but still leaving a longer play. The cuts seem designed simply to reduce the length and complexity of the text, not to adapt it to any special conditions (a smaller cast, for example); one can almost hear the editor muttering "More action and less talk."

Clearly for this reviser, the Shakespearean text has no integrity. The fluidity of the written text, the divergence between published and performing texts are historically authentic. And the claim of textual authenticity as a function of the author's hand, the folio's claim to preserve "the true original copies" becomes an issue only when the plays are printed, and are then claimed to be authors' plays, not actors' plays.

---

[7] For a detailed discussion, see my essay "Acting Scripts, Performing Texts."

In fact, the degree to which the authority of a theatrical text is that of the author will be all but impossible to determine: What kind of true original can the folio text of *Macbeth* have been? In this case (and the case can hardly be unique) "original" means that the copy is the one used by the company. The authentic text on which performances are based is the authorized text, which is not necessarily a text in the author's hand. Even authorial texts would have been far more fluid, far more unstable, than most of us, with our yearnings toward final and authoritative versions, will wish to allow. We believe that texts develop and evolve toward publication, and that publishing texts fixes them; we expend great efforts on "establishing" texts that we can then call "authentic." The claim is historically inaccurate, and blinds us to the true nature of the works we are dealing with.

Indeed, it is not even correct to say that printed books in the period fix or preserve a text. Because of the practice of making proof corrections during the course of printing, and of assembling the finished book using both corrected and uncorrected sheets indiscriminately, every copy of the Shakespeare folio is different from every other copy; the same is true, to a greater or lesser degree, of all Renaissance books. To the literary historian the differences may appear insignificant, but to anyone interested in the history of the concept of the book, the fact that such variability was not only acceptable but built into the system is of the essence.

Revision

With the reopening of the theaters at the Restoration, Shakespeare became both a classic and out of date, and the royal license to produce plays carried with it a stipulation that Shakespeare be updated, adapted to the modern theater.[8] This has been represented as more of an innovation than it was: we have seen that the revising of Shakespeare was in progress in the 1620s and before, and in fact the *Macbeth* promptbook, *c*.1640, makes a number of the notorious rationalizing changes

---

[8] See Richard Schoch and Amanda Eubanks Winkler, *Shakespeare in the Theatre: Sir William Davenant and the Duke's Company* (The Arden Shakespeare, London: Bloomsbury, 2022).

that Sir William Davenant later incorporated into his version. The real difference is that after the reopening of the theaters, Shakespeare was a text; the revised versions, "as presently performed," were published and could be compared with the plays in the folio, and critics from Dryden's time on observed, with varying degrees of indignation, that the revisions were not the same as the originals. Charles Gildon, in a critical essay appended to Nicholas Rowe's Shakespeare (1710), was especially hard on the Restoration version of *The Tempest*.

Davenant and Dryden's play, he wrote, is not only "much less perfect but infinitely more extravagant" than Shakespeare's, and the characters and incidents are much less believable. The alteration," he concludes, "has been no benefit to the original."[9] This is quite different from arguing that what is wrong with the Davenant and Dryden text is that it is inauthentic. The issue is performability or readability, and Gildon's claim is that Shakespeare's text is a better play. We will sympathize with this claim, but it is belied by 150 years of theatrical history—Davenant and Dryden's was the standard performing text of *The Tempest* until 1832—and in any case it reveals no prejudice in favor of Shakespeare. Gildon in the same essay finds Dryden's *Troilus and Cressida* and Nahum Tate's *King Lear* superior to the originals; there is nothing in the argument privileging authenticity.

A decade later Pope, revising the plays to make them more rational (i.e., more comprehensible), mystifies Gildon's straightforward claim by arguing that he was thereby restoring the Shakespearean text, removing what was inauthentic. Pope's edition was declared amateurish and ill informed by the textual scholars, which it certainly is, but the attitude it embodies is nevertheless still firmly embedded in a great deal of very respectable editorial practice. As we have seen, Camillo in *The Winter's Tale*, furiously expostulating with Leontes, has the elliptical line "I have loved thee—" (1.2.321). A number of eighteenth-century editors were disturbed by this, arguing that a courtier could not address the sovereign in the second person singular, and many modern editors continue to see the pronoun as problematic. Here quite anachronistic notions of etiquette are assumed to constitute the reality of the text, trumping a moment of great dramatic intensity.

---

[9] Nicholas Rowe, ed., The Works of Mr. *William Shakespear*, 7 vols (London, 1709-10), 7:261, 272.

I have elsewhere cited a similar point in Frank Kermode's Arden 2 edition of *The Tempest*, where a folio reading is emended with the explanation that the original "is disagreeable, being grotesque in a context which does not require grotesquerie," and therefore cannot be correct. The crux is in Ariel's song "Come unto these yellow sands"; the lines read in the folio:

> Curtsied when you have, and kist
> the wilde waves whist
>
> (1.2.376–7).

where the spirits' act of love quiets the waves. It is this that Kermode finds grotesque, and following a number of editors starting with Rowe in 1709, places a comma after "kissed," rendering the next line parenthetical. But decorum is not transhistorical; what is perfectly seemly in one age may be disagreeable in another. For the subsequent Arden 3 edition, the passage was no longer grotesque and the offending line was printed as it appears in all the seventeenth-century folios.[10]

Editors in the tradition running from, say, Samuel Johnson to George Lyman Kittredge, editors whose concept of the editorial task was the translation of the obscurities of Shakespearean verse into clear, rational prose are also arguing against the authority, if not the authenticity, of the text. The meaning lies, in these cases, in the translation, as the text lay, for Pope, in the revision. The assumption is that behind the obscure and imperfect text lies a clear and perfect one, and revealing that notional text is the editor's proper task.

The Ideal Text

The play is conceived here as a platonic idea, only imperfectly represented by its text. The conception is implicit in critical history, and even occasionally explicit. John Dennis argued in 1712 that Shakespeare

---

[10] *The Tempest*, ed. Frank Kermode, The Arden Shakespeare (Arden Shakespeare 2), note to 1.2.379. The emendation is discussed in more detail in my essay "Acting Scripts, Performing Texts." The Arden 3 edition of Virginia Mason Vaughan and Alden T. Vaughan returns to the folio punctuation—that is, the line does not end with a comma, and "waves" remains as it is in the folio, the object of "kissed." Gary Taylor's *New Oxford Shakespeare* follows Rowe, Kermode, and numerous others in emending the syntax, making "the wild waves whist" parenthetical, in this case by placing it between dashes.

wrote in haste and without the benefit of learned and tasteful advice, and that editors ought to produce the texts that Shakespeare would have written had he been able to revise.[11] Most editors have subscribed in some measure to the first half of this proposition, and few have been untouched by the second. Pope, for example, assumes that the infelicities and obscurities were imposed on the text by actors or early printers, and it is these that he undertakes to remove or revise as inauthentic. Pope is thus able to claim, unlike Dennis, that the improved and rationalized text is not what Shakespeare ought to have written but what he actually wrote, but Pope's editorial practice of rewriting whatever does not seem to him "Shakespearean" implicitly endorses Dennis's claim that the ideal text is the authentic one. The claim sounds outrageously condescending to modern ears, but in fact it is at heart also a very modern, even postmodern, claim: The text is not a function of the author; the author is a function of the text.

Shakespeare is, to these eighteenth-century critics, the supreme playwright, the most perfect exemplar in English of the art. It is the texts, therefore, that must be perfect. Shakespeare's perfection derives from the perfection of the text, and that is supplied by the editor. Modern claims are much more modest, but, as the Kermode example indicates, they often share Pope's basic assumptions—for Kermode, Shakespeare had to be rescued from grotesquerie. Stanley Wells, the general editor of the 1986 Oxford Shakespeare (which has now been superseded by Gary Taylor's *New Oxford Shakespeare*), recommended to the editors of the individual plays that they emend in the case of palpable errors, by which he meant not simply printers' errors but places where it may be assumed that Shakespeare would have acquiesced in the correction if the need for it had been pointed out to him.[12] Our editions are to preserve, that is, not what Shakespeare wrote but what he ought (or "really intended") to have written. Wells had in mind what we might call trivial cases (confusions in characters' names, for example) though even here what is trivial to one generation or group of readers may be of

---

[11] John Dennis, "On the Genius and Writings of Shakespear," letter 3, in D. Nichol Smith, ed., *Eighteenth-Century Essays on Shakespeare* (2nd edition, Oxford: Oxford University Press, 1963), pp. 39–42.

[12] Stanley Wells, from "The Oxford Shakespeare Editorial Procedures," November 1978, p. 15. This is a mimeographed handbook supplied to the editors of volumes in the series.

the essence to another. Ben Jonson apparently talked Shakespeare into making just such a change in *Julius Caesar*, pointing out the illogic of a line of Caesar's that he gives as "Caesar did never wrong, but with just cause."[13] The passage as it appears in the printed text is "Know, Caesar doth not wrong, nor without cause | Will he be satisfied" (3.1.47–48). Few modern readers will prefer the revised version, which seems to us to have edited out the point of the line, the ambiguities of the concept "Caesar." In the same way, Wells's simple errors might turn out to be of the essence to a psychoanalytic critic, a crucial key to the mind behind the text.

But what does a play represent? However authentic our texts are assumed to be, they clearly represent something more than the playwright's mind. Shakespeare's plays have most often been held to be transparent, vehicles for the representation of, say, human nature or history; what is authentic in them, Shakespeare's perfection, lies in what is represented, something behind the play and beyond it that the play brings to life. The ability of Shakespearean texts to realize a recognizable version of human psychology has generally been felt, from the earliest commentators onward, to be beyond praise; but in fact the plays have always required a good deal of help in this respect, whether from revisers and elucidators or from actors, directors, and stage designers. Indeed, Shakespearean texts, as we have seen, have been found inadequate to the demands of theatrical representation as far back as our evidence goes, and they have always required, in varying degrees at various times, revisions, cuts, and additions.

The Changeable Text

In fact, one of the most remarkable aspects of the theatrical medium is its ability to comprehend the widest variety of versions of a dramatic text within the concept of a single play. Davenant and Dryden's *Tempest* does not look much like *The Tempest* of the folio: it has a male ingenu parallel to Miranda named Hippolito, a young man who has never seen a woman; Miranda has been supplied with a sister, Dorinda; Sycorax has become Caliban's sister; Ariel has a girlfriend named Milcha; and

---

[13] From Ben Jonson, "Explorata; or, Discoveries," in *The Cambridge Ben Jonson*, 7: 522.

only about a third of the dialogue bears any relation to the original text at all. This, in one form or another, was the standard performing version of *The Tempest* until 1832, and, despite critical protests from Gildon to Hazlitt, both it and the scholarly text on the bookshelf of every literate household were Shakespeare's *Tempest*.

Nor is the situation significantly different today: Modern directors feel no less free than Henry Irving, John Philip Kemble, Colley Cibber, or Sir William Davenant to cut or rewrite the masque, assign Miranda's denunciation of Caliban to Prospero, or replace the epilogue with Prospero's speech as he dismisses the masque, "Our revels now are ended . . . ." The concept of *The Tempest* has never been limited to the original text. A Shakespeare play on the stage has always involved other intentions than the author's, and it really does not need to be argued that, despite editorial claims for textual authenticity, editions of the plays, from the earliest quartos on, embody nonauthorial intentions as well. These are performances too, concerned with fixing the text, in both senses, in the interests of particular interpretations. The history of realizations of the text, that is, is the history of the text.

| 5 |

The Jonson Folios

When Ben Jonson, in his mid-forties, produced his *Workes* in folio (1616) he was in effect declaring himself a classic author while he was still alive. Although most folio *Works* were historical, philosophical, or scientific, and the authors were long dead, there was a recent literary precedent for Jonson: the first folio collection by a living English writer was Samuel Daniel's *Works*, published in 1601. But Jonson did not take Daniel as his model. He took instead the great sixteenth-century continental editions of Greek and Roman authors, especially the dramatists. Jonson duly placed his plays first in the collection, to some surprise and disapproval: ancient plays were classics, but modern plays were popular entertainment. Hence this witty exchange:

> *To Mr. Ben Johnson, demanding the reason why he call'd his playes works.*
>   Pray tell me *Ben*, where doth the mystery lurke,
>   What others call a play, you call a worke.

Plays for the popular stage were not "works." An admirer refuted the critique, however, not by defending plays, but by making Jonson an exception:

> *Thus answer'd by a friend in Mr. Johnsons defence.*
>   The authors friend thus for the author sayes.
>   *Bens* plays are works, when others works are plaies.[1]

[1] *Wits Recreations* (1640), nos 269 and 270, fol. G3^v.

Daniel's folio *Works* had also included plays, but they were not plays for the popular stage; moreover, Daniel was far less contentious than Jonson, and did not attract hostility as Jonson did.

Classical Jonson

Even the early quartos of Jonson's plays look like editions of the classics, divided into acts and scenes, and with a good deal of paratextual material. There were precedents: Daniel's *Cleopatra* (1594) was provided with an Argument and a cast of characters, and is divided into acts and scenes; the Countess of Pembroke's *Antonie* (1592), reissued in 1595 under the title *Antonius*, had been published in a similar fashion, as had Thomas Kyd's *Cornelia* (1595). These were based on French dramas by Robert Garnier, obviously classical imitations, and the publishers may have been imitating the French editions; but Kyd's *Soliman and Perseda* (1592) and Marlowe's hugely popular *Tamburlaine* (1590) are divided into acts and scenes, and *Tamburlaine* explicitly says it has been revised to appeal to readers. The title page of Jonson's earliest quarto, *Every Man Out of His Humour* (1600), declares that it includes "more than hath been Publickely Spoken or Acted. With the severall Character of every Person"—there is a great deal more to the play in this form than you could see in the theater. The book enabled Jonson to keep control of the play, as he could not do in the theater, extending the action, giving instructions for interpretation, managing the reader as he could not manage the actors.

Much in Jonson's printed texts, moreover, is addressed solely to readers: In addition to the numerous congratulatory poems prefacing the play quartos, from Jonson's own pen there are the extensive character sketches in the *dramatis personae* of *Every Man Out of His Humour*, the prefatory "needfull notes" and marginal citation of sources in *Sejanus*, the addresses to the universities of Oxford and Cambridge in *Volpone* and to readers of *The Alchemist* urging them to be understanders, the two epistles in *Catiline* "To the Reader in Ordinarie" and "To the Reader extraordinary"—Jonson, of course, conceives the latter to be his true audience. Perhaps most striking are the acrostic titles prefaced to *Volpone* and *The Alchemist*, which show Jonson being playful in a way that could only be manifest in writing, and that, moreover, was not manifest when the book was read aloud. And as "more than hath been Publickely Spoken or Acted" reveals, the printed texts contain much that was not included in the play in the theater—how much there is no way of knowing, but anyone who has worked on a production of a Jonson play knows how much cutting is required to return it to the stage. That is true of the surviving texts of Shakespeare plays too, as it must be of any play revised for publication where all that has survived is the published version.

Jonson Revising

Jonson was significantly involved in the production of his folio *Workes*, not only proofreading but rewriting while the book was in the press—the book contains over 2,500 press changes (the Shakespeare folio, which includes more text, has about 500). Jonson also rewrote one play completely, changing the setting of *Every Man In His Humour* from Italy to England, and thus modernizing it into a London city comedy; he added substantial passages to his court comedy *Cynthia's Revels* and his classical comedy *Poetaster*; included previously unpublished texts such as those of *Epicoene* and the court masques performed between 1609 and 1615 in the volume; and revised his wedding masque *Hymenaei* to conceal the fact that the couple being celebrated were the Earl and Countess of Essex, who, by 1616, had dissolved their union in a scandalous divorce. He suppressed the ending of his *Epistle To Elizabeth, Countess of Rutland* (*Forest* 12), with the notation that "The rest is lost"—the conclusion, which survives in manuscript, predicted the birth of a son, but it had become clear shortly after Rutland's marriage to the Countess, Sir Philip Sidney's daughter, that the Earl was impotent, and it was a singularly unhappy union. Jonson refashioned his civic pageant for King James's entry into London to make it appear part of the coronation festivities, claiming, in effect, that he was working for the king and court, not for the London mercantile companies. The folio for Jonson thus not only claimed classic status for his work, but revised his career to refresh the work, remove embarrassments, and elevate the social status of his patrons. As the Cambridge editors sum it up:

> Jonson's grouping of the texts into plays, poems, and masques further imposes a narrative onto his career. It implies that he had moved

effortlessly out of the playhouse and into the worlds of patronage poetry and crown service, and it carefully locates the poetry in a personal space between the more public arenas of theatre and court.[2]

The Play as Text

"Containing more than hath been Publickely Spoken or Acted." The published text of the play was not the same as the play on the stage. It began as a script, instructions for performance, continually revised by the performers, but ended as literature, initially with the author in control, but thereafter subjected to centuries of editorial effort. The editorial effort was always designed to establish a correct text, whereas the text in the theater was never "established," but was endlessly malleable. As we have seen, Humphrey Moseley, issuing the plays of Beaumont and Fletcher in folio in 1647, is explicit about the difference between the play as script and the play as book. Here again is the passage:

> When these *Comedies* and *Tragedies* were presented on the Stage, the *Actours* omitted some *Scenes* and Passages (with the *Authour's* consent) as occasion led them; ... But now you have both All that was *Acted*, and all that was not; even the perfect full Originalls without the least mutilation; So that were the *Authours* living ... they themselves would challenge neither more nor lesse then what is here published ...[3]

The stage, for Moseley, "mutilates" the perfect original, which is what comes from the author's pen. The play on the stage is a collaboration between authors and performers; whereas in the book, Moseley insists, it is wholly the author's. But as the examples of *Tamburlaine* and *The Spanish Tragedy* acknowledge, the play-as-book has gone through an editorial process, sometimes quite radical, to render it a text for readers. Moseley's claim conceals that process—and of course there is no knowing how much editorial intervention Moseley's texts went through.

---

[2] Cambridge Ben Jonson, 1:lxvi.
[3] *Comedies and Tragedies Written by Francis Beaumont and John Fletcher* (1647), fol. A4^r.

Jonson was clearly significantly involved in the printing of those of his plays that were issued in quarto; but for the folio, even plays that were not radically revised (as *Every Man In His Humour*, *Cynthia's Revels*, and *Poetaster* were) had marginal notes added to indicate stage action (e.g., in *The Alchemist*, "*Shee catcheth out* Face *his sword: and breakes Subtle's glasse*," "*Upon Subtles entry they disperse*," "*A great crack and noise within*," "*Subtle falls downe as in a swoune*"). In fact, the plays in folio were throughout subtly different from the plays in quarto. While *Volpone* retains its dedication to the two universities, of its ten dedicatory poems only three have been preserved, and moved to the beginning of the whole collected volume, thereby making them seem testimonials to the excellence of the folio, rather than of the play. The harangue to the reader was deleted from *The Alchemist*, and all the learned marginalia citing the historical sources of *Sejanus* have been replaced by notes indicating stage action (*"They whisper," "Drusus passeth by," "He turnes to Sejanus clyents,"*) so that the folio's *Sejanus* is theatrical in a way the quarto's is not.

From Script to Book

Jonson may be taken to represent the final phase of the development from script to book, the playwright who takes back control of his plays from the actors, revises them for publication and includes a whole range of devices for directing the response of the readers, as he could never do with audiences. The devices are all things you never find in Shakespeare: dedications, cast lists with descriptions of the characters, a list of the actors including Shakespeare (though maddeningly for us, no indication of what roles they played), introductory epistles, prologues, summaries, choric characters who stand in for the author, sometimes even marginal explanatory notes. Jonson keeps a very tight rein on the plays, which are not open in the way Shakespeare's are. In particular, they are not open-ended, in the way that Shakespeare often introduces some unexpected concluding twist that seems to require the play to continue—in *Love's Labour's Lost* the ladies refuse to settle into the marriages the whole play has been moving toward, but impose a year's trial on the men; *Twelfth Night*'s concluding weddings cannot take place until Malvolio has been mollified and Viola's women's clothes returned, but Malvolio has stormed out of the play swearing revenge; *All's Well That Ends Well* concludes with the ambiguous observation that "All yet seems well." But Jonson's endings are neat and definitive; so much so, that we distrust them—those neat conclusions simply do not exhaust, or even contain, the energy of the drama.

And then, in the plays as published, there are the beginnings: Consider the effect of the defensive preface to the Universities in *Volpone*— what does it have to do with the play, and does it have any effect on it? Jonson wrote the play very fast—five weeks, he says—and it was first performed at the Globe in April 1606. It then went on the road, and was performed in Oxford and Cambridge: Jonson makes much more of this than of the Globe performance, or indeed, of the king's patronage. To judge from the dedication, the university was the audience he cared most about, the audience he wanted to justify himself to. Similarly, *The Alchemist* was intended for performance at the Blackfriars in autumn 1610, but the London theaters were closed because of plague, so the play opened in September in Oxford—the choice of Oxford rather than, say, York or Canterbury surely was not accidental.

The only Shakespearean analogue to this appeal to the universities through performance is the first quarto of *Hamlet* (1603), which advertises on its title page that it has been performed in Oxford and Cambridge; and the only other Shakespeare play that makes the same sorts of academic claims as *Hamlet*, with its philosophical musings, is *Troilus and Cressida*, a play that its preface claims was "never stal'd with the stage, never clapperclawd with the palmes of the vulger." It is probably easier to see what the special attraction of *The Alchemist* would have been for a university audience than what the attraction of *Volpone* would have been; though for *The Alchemist*, the academic audience might have been divided, part assuming that Jonson was indicting only fraudulent alchemy, and part believing that alchemy as such was fraudulent. Perhaps Jonson merely saw in university audiences a group that would understand his classicism, the relation of his plays to those of Aristophanes, Plautus, and Terence—here was a playwright who bridged the gap between learned and popular drama. Drama was part of the university curriculum, both as texts and in performance.

From the late seventeenth century *Volpone* and *The Alchemist* have been Jonson's most perennially popular plays, but with their very tight structures they are in fact uncharacteristic. In these two plays (as in the two tragedies Jonson chose to preserve, *Sejanus* and *Catiline*) one may see the structure as classical, and assume that that is its attraction for Jonson; but taking the career as a whole, one may wonder whether this kind of structure was really natural to him: think of *Every Man Out of His Humour* or *Cynthia's Revels*. His next play after the Senecan *Catiline* was *Bartholomew Fair*, where much of the dramatic tension comes from the effort to keep the fecundity of Jonson's imagination under control; and that is the case with all the later plays. The tendency of Jonson's verse, even in *Volpone*, *The Alchemist*, and the two tragedies, is always toward aggregation, *copia*, not toward compression or epigram. *Bartholomew Fair* is a great mass of matter, and in prose. *Epicoene*, the play immediately preceding *The Alchemist*, also in prose, is all about the problems of keeping life under control, finding a way of managing intrusions and distractions, epitomized in women. This is what *Volpone* and *The Alchemist* are about too, only the controlling figures are successful because they determine how to make money out of the intruders, whereas in *Epicoene* the intruders are doing the bilking.

Jonson's notion of structure in the two "classical" comedies appears supremely rational. The play is a machine. The characters relate to each other as gears mesh in a machine. Initially the pleasure the play provides is the pleasure of watching the machine run, smoothly, ingeniously, just as the manufacturer claims. But then the pleasure changes: something goes wrong. One of the gears fails to mesh—decides not to mesh: Corvino arrives too early; Subtle and Face have a fight. In this case, we have really arrived in the middle of the structure (or to put it in an appropriately classical form, "we plunge *in medias res*"). The pleasure then is in watching the attempt to keep the machine from falling apart. This structure is largely self-contained. The villainy of *Volpone* is exposed not because the justices determine the truth, but because the villains outfox themselves, go too far. *The Alchemist* concludes simply because the plague ends and the master returns; there is no retribution—on the contrary, Lovewit the master is the big winner; his wily, terminally dishonest but faithful servant delivers him a rich widow to marry. One may even see *Sejanus* and *Catiline* as essentially comic, in the way *Richard III* is (and an early tragedy that Jonson chose not to preserve was *Richard Crookback*): the pleasure is in watching the villainous manipulations, and then the tables turned upon the villains, who get what the plays present them as deserving.

Even in the most tightly organized of Jonson's plays, the structure keeps pausing for linguistic displays—these are often the great moments: Volpone's opening hymn to his gold, Sir Epicure Mammon's celebration of what he will achieve with the Philosopher's Stone, Wittipol's beautiful wooing speech in *The Devil Is an Ass*:

> Think,
> All beauty doth not last until the autumn.
> You grow old while I tell you this.
>
> (1.6.128–31)

The Masque

Criticism as far back as Jonson's own time has focussed on the audacity of his inclusion of his plays in his *Workes*, but even more striking is the inclusion of the masques and entertainments. This, as we have seen, sometimes involved outright misrepresentation, to make the event celebrated sound grander than it was; but there is also a good deal of revision and suppression, to conceal or remove things that by 1616 had become embarrassments. I have already cited the example of *Hymenaei*, produced in 1606 for the wedding of the Earl and Countess of Essex. Ten years later not only had the couple gone through a notorious divorce, but the bride and her new husband were in the Tower, accused of complicity in the murder of Sir Thomas Overbury. For the quarto in 1606, a principal attraction had been precisely the original couple's names, announced on the title page: "the auspicious celebrating of the Marriage-*union*, between *Robert*, Earl of *Essex*, and the Lady *Frances*, second Daughter to the most noble Earle of *Suffolke*." The folio gives no indication of the occasion.

Clearly Jonson invested a great deal in his masque texts, documents of his association with the aristocratic world; but transforming a masque into a book necessarily omitted far more than transforming the text of a play did. The text of a masque constituted only the smallest part of the spectator's experience; it might comprise ten or fifteen pages, but the entertainment typically took several hours, and consisted primarily of dancing and music. To start with a definition, a masque, in the period, was most simply an entertainment including masked performers, primarily dancers. In its most characteristic form, it was a private entertainment that related to its audience in a manner significantly different from drama: It was basically celebratory; it was about the group it entertained, and always ended by including them in the fiction. In court masques the usual way of bringing this about was to conclude the work with a grand dance, called the revels; the masquers descended from the stage and took partners from among the spectators, so that what the audience began by watching they ended by becoming. The dancers were the aristocrats; speaking roles in the introductory antimasque, what Jonson calls "a foil or false masque," were typically taken by professional actors, who were banished as the work moved to its climax.[4] It was, then, more of a game than a show, an expression of aristocratic identity and privilege, with the masks providing a degree of freedom, even if only notional, from the constraints of place, office, and self. The masks were not designed as part of the costumes, which were very elaborate and splendid; the masks were uniform and neutral. They were typically made of leather covered in black velvet or silk, and were secured by a bead sewed to the mouth area held between the teeth—the masks were thus easily removed for conversation or dining.

Both Henry VIII and Queen Elizabeth loved to dance, and masked dances and entertainments were a staple of court culture throughout the sixteenth century; but the form was only systematized and theorized under James I and Charles I. Initially the most important patrons were not the king, but Queen Anne and Prince Henry. The collection of masques preserved in the folio gives a strong sense of the changing shape of the form, from emblematic pageant to miniature symbolic drama. But the texts really tell us very little—they mostly tell us about intentions and purposes and meanings. They are especially unforthcoming in cases where things do not go as planned, which culturally are the most interesting cases. Thomas Campion is almost alone in

---

[4] The definition of the antimasque is from the introductory epistle to *The Masque of Queens*, 1609, line 9; Jonson credits its inclusion to the suggestion of Queen Anne. The only masque in which aristocrats took speaking parts was *The Gypsies Metamorphosed*, commissioned by Buckingham for him to star in and performed three times in 1621. The best accounts of this extraordinary production are Dale B. J. Randall, *Jonson's Gypsies Unmasked* (Durham, NC: Duke University Press, 1975) and Martin Butler, "'We are one mans all': Jonson's 'The Gipsies Metamorphosed,'" *The Yearbook of English Studies*, 21 (1991), 253–73.

acknowledging failure—in this case the failure of the scenic machinery in *Lord Hay's Masque* (1607), "either by the simplicity, negligence, or conspiracy of the painter,"⁵ as he puts it, thereby exculpating himself, but at the same time acknowledging how little control the text has over the performance. Our evidence in such instances is almost invariably the evidence of report and gossip, which is characteristically more interested in performance than intention, performers than scripts, audiences than performers.

Sir John Harington's satiric account of a masque about Solomon and the Queen of Sheba, devised for the entertainment of James I and Christian IV of Denmark, Queen Anne's brother, in 1606, is a case in point. It has become a touchstone for the indecorum of the Jacobean court, and since the text of the masque does not survive, Harington's letter has in effect become the masque. In fact, the performance may well have been a fiction invented by Harington to satirize the Jacobean court, whose manners he despised; there are no other references to it, though Christian's visit is quite well documented.⁶ Indeed, if it is a fantasy, the fantasy is as much the creation of a boorish audience as of an inept performance.

Harington's account is well known. Here I quote rather more of it than usual, since I want to focus on some things that are generally overlooked:

> after dinner the representation of Solomon his Temple and the coming of the Queen of Sheba was made, or (as I may better say) was meant to have been made, before their Majesties, by device of the Earl of Salisbury and others.

(Note that credit for the "device" belongs to the patrons, not the poet and architect).

> But, alass!... The lady who did play the Queens part did carry most precious gifts to both their majesties; but, forgetting the steppes arising to the canopy, overset her casket into his Danish Majesties lap,

---

⁵ Thomas Campion, *The discription of a maske, presented before the Kinges Maiestie at White-Hall, on Twelfth Night last in honour of the Lord Hayes, and his bride...* (London, 1607), marginal note to fol. C2ᵛ.

⁶ Martin Butler makes the suggestion in *The Stuart Court Masque and Political Culture* (Cambridge: Cambridge University Press, 2008), p. 126.

and fell at his feet, tho I rather think it was in his face. Much was the hurry and confusion; cloths and napkins were at hand, to make all clean. His Majesty then got up, and woud dance with the Queen of Sheba; but he fell down and humbled himself before her, and was carried to an inner chamber and laid on a bed of state; which was not a little defiled with the presents of the Queen which had been bestowed on his garments; such as wine, cream, jelly, beverage, cakes, spices, and other good matters.

The account continues to tell how most of the speakers bungled their parts through incompetence or drunkenness. King James, moreover—this is worth stressing—was decidedly uncooperative:

Victory, in bright armor ... presented a rich sword to the King, who did not accept it, but put it by with his hand; and ... did endeavour to make suit to the King. But ... after much lamentable utterance, she was led away like a silly captive and laid to sleep in the outer steps of the anti-chamber.

Harington concludes that "I neer did see such lack of good order, discretion, and sobriety, as I have now done."[7]

This is all that survives of a masque embodying King James's most deeply felt persona, the Solomonic monarch, and the only masque recorded from his reign on a biblical subject. If the masque was real, not imagined by Harington, James could not have been ignorant of the text. Why did the king refuse the sword of Victory? He must have known it was to be presented. Was he, like Harington, simply so offended by the indecorum that he withdrew from the game? Or was there a deeper meaning that Harington missed, even if he was inventing the whole thing: the pacifist king refusing the martial image? Or was this even perhaps part of the show, included by Harington's monarchical imagination? Even in masques where nothing goes wrong, what spectators see often differs significantly from what inventors intend, nor are the implications of the work limited, or even determined, by the inventors' intentions.

---

[7] The letter, to an unidentified Mr. Secretary Barlow—clearly not any of the Jacobean-era Barlows recorded in the DNB—was first printed by Harington's descendant Henry Harington in *Nugae Antiquae* (2 vols, London, 1769–75), vol. 2, pp. 133–5. It can also be found in John Nichols, *The Progresses, Processions, and Magnificent Festivities, of King James the First* ... (4 vols, London, 1828), 2:72–4.

Jonson's, Daniel's and Campion's texts describe—or prescribe—a court that moves in perfect order, like the movement of the spheres; the dancing is clearly the central element. Andrew Sabol, who did more than anyone to rescue the ephemeral music of this most ephemeral form, said of the dances that "the masquers function always as an identically accoutred group, moving simultaneously in sober splendor."[8] This view of the masque can certainly be derived from Jonson's or Campion's or Daniel's texts. But if we look a little further, we get a different picture. From Inigo Jones's costume designs and his annotations to them we learn how much freedom the royal and noble participants in these supreme assertions of artistocratic community and independence had in the creation of their own costumes, and thus of how they were presented. They paid for the costumes; their own dressmakers and tailors made them. The costumes were based on Jones's drawings, but the aristocratic masquer adapted the final outfit to his or her own taste. A startling piece of evidence is preserved in the material relating to Jonson's masque *Hymenaei*, performed in 1606. Jonson's text describes the ladies' garments in detail: the masquers were to be identically dressed, in a very elaborate costume with a double skirt. The outer layer was to be of carnation striped with silver, the inner of light blue cloth-of-silver laced with gold. Now it happens that three ladies who danced in this masque had their portraits painted in costume. Two accord closely with Jonson's description; the third, however, shows not a double but a single skirt.[9] That was how this noble masquer preferred to appear. I cite Sabol's account not because it seems to me egregiously incorrect (though it does), but because it remains so completely within the terms provided by the poets' texts. If we look beyond the texts, we get quite a different picture. Jones made the costume designs, but he was an employee, working to order, paid not to dictate but to realize the intentions of his employers.

Here is another example of aristocratic independence: When at the performance of Jonson's *Love Restored* on Twelfth Night 1612, the lords went to take out the ladies to dance the revels, John Chamberlain

---

[8] Andrew Sabol, *Four Hundred Songs and Dances from the Stuart Masque* (Providence: Brown University Press, 1977), p. 12.

[9] For reproductions of the portraits see Stephen Orgel and Roy Strong, *Inigo Jones* (London and Berkeley: Sotheby and University of California Press, 1973), 2 vols, 1:104, 114.

reports, "beginning with [the ladies] of Essex and Cranbourne, they were refused, [which set an] example to the rest, so that [the lords] were fain to dance alone and make court to one another."[10]

The only way we know about what must have been a real fiasco is from Chamberlain's letter: Jonson is understandably silent about it. Gossip here is of the essence. At this remove, it is very difficult to know what the problem was. The Countess of Essex (who was not yet the notorious divorcée) and Viscountess Cranbourne were sisters, Frances and Catherine Howard, daughters of the Earl of Suffolk—stars of James's court, daughters of a powerful and very influential peer. Suffolk apparently was embarrassed by their behavior, but since the rest of the ladies followed their lead, the problem they perceived cannot have been theirs alone. It has been suggested, plausibly, that the lords, most of whom were Scots, were seen by the Howard ladies as upstarts and insufficiently aristocratic, and if this is correct, the incident gives us a good insight into the limits of protocol and the extent of courtly privilege and independence at such events. But this cannot be the whole story: What happens when the audience refuses to play its part? The work was jointly sponsored by the king and Prince Henry, and the Scottish masquers were members of their households, so the ladies were offending not only the déclassé lords, but their royal patrons as well. One can imagine circumstances in which such behavior would have been considered deeply disruptive, even perhaps treasonable—Cordelia's behavior at the opening of *King Lear*—but if we understand Chamberlain correctly (the letter is not entirely legible) all the apologies were directed at the mortified parent, Suffolk; Chamberlain says nothing about the reaction of the king and prince. In short, the implications of this affair seem more private than public. And yet, the whole point of the masque—any masque—was precisely that public assertion of aristocratic solidarity: everybody joins in the game celebrating the glories of the crown and court. But even the gossips seem to be silent about what happens when they refuse. Is this because nothing happens, or is the lacuna simply in our evidence—or in what we must, perforce, treat as evidence?

---

[10] *Letters of John Chamberlain*, ed. Norman E. McClure (2 vols, Philadelphia: American Philosophical Society, 1939), 1:328. Some bits have been supplied—the letter is not entirely legible. See Martin Butler's discussion of the incident in *The Stuart Court Masque*, pp. 205–7.

A somewhat different kind of example is offered by *Pleasure Reconciled to Virtue* (1618). This looks to us, from the text and the few surviving designs, like one of Jones's most ingenious scenic inventions, and it includes some of Jonson's best masque poetry. Both poetry and stagecraft, however, were declared unimpressive by those contemporary spectators whose reactions are preserved; and indeed, neither poetry nor stagecraft was central to the experience of the original audience—what remains to us of the masque, the text and three drawings, represents only the smallest part of the evening's entertainment. It was the dances that mattered most, especially to King James, the crucial member of the Jacobean audience, who particularly enjoyed watching the revels. On this occasion, the royal favorite George Villiers, later Duke of Buckingham, was the star. The Venetian envoy reported that when the dancing was about to end, the king broke out in a rage, shouting (in the account, in Italian) "What did you bring me here for? Devil take you all, dance!" upon which Villiers, recently ennobled as Marquis of Buckingham, lept up and gave an impromptu performance of astonishing virtuosity, and thereby restored the king's good humor.[11]

Dancing of one kind or another occupied most of the time a court masque took to perform; a text of fifteen pages or so would normally occupy several hours in production, and the choreography and music were quite as carefully planned as the poetry, costumes, and stagecraft. The masquers themselves rehearsed their choreographed dances for weeks. Dance in the instance just described, moreover, is not simply a way of pleasing the king; it is more sigificantly a way of managing him, and for Buckingham in his rise to favor and power his skill at this courtly accomplishment constituted a potent political talent.

The most compelling and effective element of these entertainments is thus lost to us. While the political aspect of court masques and ballets has been clear for decades, the specifically political content of the dances has only begun to be investigated more recently.[12] The relation

---

[11] Busino's account is in the Archives of St. Mark's, Venice. It is quoted and translated in Orgel and Strong, *Inigo Jones*, 1:279–84. See also Martin Butler's introduction to the masque in the Cambridge Ben Jonson, 5:309ff.

[12] See Mark Franko, *Dance as Text: Ideologies of the Baroque Body* (revised edition, Oxford: Oxford University Press, 2015). Barbara Ravelhofer, *The Early Stuart Masque: Dance, Costume and Music* (Oxford: Oxford University Press, 2006), gives a richly contextual account of production and performance. The collection *The Politics of the Stuart*

of dance to text is one that is always in question, and sometimes directly adversarial, two theatrical elements that were either in collaboration or conflict, but always basically independent of each other. Dance has a subversive potential that is only imperfectly restrained by the forms of drama and conventional theater.

Dance is in one sense always subversive in court masques because the text is the monarch's; in courtly forms, as in the country as a whole, royal authority expressed itself through control of the word. But dancing is both non-verbal and an aristocratic prerogative, one of the defining features of the social elite that surrounded the monarch, and it could only partly and intermittently be contained by the royal will. (It is to the point that James did not participate in the dancing.) In this context, Frances and Catherine Howard's refusal to dance, and Villiers's impromptu performance, are not flukes but of the essence, assertions of aristocratic independence in the very presence of sovereign authority.

Masques were not simply occasions for court dances, and their issues could be significantly politicized. Thus Jonson's masque for 1623, *Time Vindicated*, staged the king's position in the continuing debate over the right of subjects to criticize the monarch's policies; and that of 1624, *Neptune's Triumph for the Return of Albion*, written to celebrate Prince Charles's return from Spain, where he had unsuccessfully wooed the Infanta, could not be performed because both the French and Spanish ambassadors had to be invited, but could not be invited together. Jonson's solution to the increasing marginalization of his texts was to theorize the masque and declare poetry its soul—the ephemeral body, the spectacle and the dancing, was the physical, and therefore mortal, element. But as Inigo Jones's expertise in art and architecture became increasingly indispensable to the court and aristocracy, Jonson found himself less and less in demand, especially after he was incapacitated by a series of strokes in the 1620s.

Jonson's last masques for the court were *Love's Triumph Through Callipolis* and *Chloridia*, the king's and queen's masques respectively, performed and published in 1631; these were also the first masques of

---

Court Masque, ed. David Bevington and Peter Holbrook (Cambridge: Cambridge University Press, 1998) includes a number of relevant essays, especially Barbara Ravelhofer, "'Virgin wax' and 'hairy men-monsters': Unstable movement Codes in the Stuart Masque" and David Lindley, "The Politics of Music in the Masque."

Charles I's reign, six years after he ascended the throne—Charles had ended the Jacobean tradition of an annual masque at the new year. Jonson published no more new work, and died in 1637. A second edition of *Catiline* appeared in 1635. The play, which had been unsuccessful on its first performance in 1611, was popular when it was revived in the 1630s, and was the most widely cited of Jonson's works in the seventeenth century—the political relevance throughout the period of this play about political dissension culminating in civil war is obvious. The new edition, published in 1635, declares on its title page that it was "now acted by His Majesty's Servants with great applause." Three plays, *Bartholomew Fair*, *The Devil Is an Ass*, and *The Staple of News* had been printed in 1631, a miniature second folio, but the volume was never issued—it is very carelessly printed, and Jonson was unhappy with the printer—and the corrected sheets were eventually used in the folio of 1640–41. The play *The New Inn* was performed in 1629, according to Jonson "never acted but most negligently play'd." It was reportedly hissed from the stage, and prompted Jonson's second *Ode to Himself*, "Come, leave the loathèd stage . . ." It was published in 1631 in octavo, with a long, aggrieved preface to the reader, who is declared the play's true audience. It was not included in the 1640–41 folio, presumably because copies of the octavo were still unsold—it first appeared in a collected Jonson in the folio of 1692. Jonson did not in fact subsequently eschew the stage; *The Tale of a Tub*, his last play staged in his lifetime, dates from 1633 (it was not published separately, but is included in the 1640–41 folio). Aside from the two masques of 1631 and *The New Inn*, his work from the 1630s circulated only in manuscript.

But this work included several vitriolic epigrams aimed at Inigo Jones. Not surprisingly, they were not admired at court, and Jonson's friend James Howell blamed them for Jonson's loss of favor. He wrote Jonson, "If your spirit will not let you retract, yet you shall do well to repress any more copies of the satire, for to deal plainly with you, you have lost some ground at court by it, and as I hear from a good hand, the King who hath so great judgement in poetry (as in all other things) is not well pleased therewith."[13] The letter was written in 1631, but Jonson's attacks on Jones continued: in *The Tale of a Tub* Jones was initially satirized as Vitruvius Hoop; the censor ordered these passages deleted,

[13] Cambridge Ben Jonson, 6:375.

but Jonson merely changed the character's name to In-and-In Medlay, suggesting a motley and intrusive figure. The play was performed at court, but was not a success. In the next year Jonson presented Jones as Iniquo Vitruvius in his last masque *Love's Welcome at Bolsover*, staged for his patron William Cavendish, later Duke of Newcastle, for a royal visit to his recently completed castle at Bolsover in 1634. Clearly Jonson was beyond advice, but Jones was equally adamant, complaining that his name was not listed first on the title page of *Love's Triumph Through Callipolis* (which names the inventors as Ben Jonson and Inigo Jones)—*Chloridia*, published at the same time, lists no inventors.

Certainly Jonson was disappointed and angry when his plays were not popular on stage and his masques were not admired. But increasingly he regarded his true audience as readers.

| 6 |

Classical Models

From the latter half of the sixteenth century classical drama was a potent model for English drama, especially English drama in print. But what did classical imply, and what should classical drama look like, both on stage and in print? The first surviving plays in English on Roman models were the Senecan *Gorboduc* and the Terentian/ Plautine comedies *Ralph Roister Doister*, *Gammer Gurton's Needle*, and *Jack Juggler*; but in their printed editions they look entirely English, printed in the black letter typeface that was standard for works in the vernacular, rather than the roman font that was used for texts in Latin—plays only began to be regularly printed in roman type in the 1590s. Moreover, as we have seen, *Gorboduc*, with its interludes of dumb shows, in performance would not have looked Senecan at all.

But let us begin with what was deemed properly classical. For modern drama, the essential ancient model of tragedy has been Sophocles's *Oedipus Tyrannos*, largely under the influence of Freud. The drama of unperceived guilt, forbidden desire, and revelation has seemed to us to have a universal application. Moreover, Aristotle in the *Poetics* uses the play as a model for tragedy, confirming its timeless relevance. To the Renaissance, however, the Oedipus story looked quite different from the version we derive from Sophocles and Freud. Its center was not the supplanting of the father in the mother's bed, but the defeat of the murderous sphinx through the solving of a riddle—a characteristic gloss on Oedipus from 1613 is "a riddle-reader of Thebes": that was the essential

Oedipus.[1] In fact, Sophocles's play was not widely known in Renaissance England (nor was Aristotle's *Poetics*). Versions of the story were based principally on the mythographers, and the dramatic source was Seneca's *Oedipus*, not Sophocles's. Sophocles came late to England: The first English translation of a Sophocles play was Charles Wase's *Electra*, published in 1649, with a dedication to Charles I's daughter Elizabeth—in the year of the king's execution, the play had an obvious political relevance. The first English edition of the Greek text of Sophocles was not published until 1668; there was no English translation of Aristotle's *Poetics* until 1705, and even that was based on a French version. The first complete English Sophocles appeared only in the eighteenth century.[2]

English Seneca

Seneca, however, was studied by English schoolboys throughout the sixteenth century, and translations of the plays were published from the mid-century onward. It was Seneca who provided the model for tragedy. Seneca's *Oedipus* is quite different from Sophocles's. In Sophocles, Oedipus is arrogant and imperious, and only gradually learns of his responsibility for the plague that is afflicting Thebes; but Seneca's Oedipus is tremulous, wracked with guilt from the outset, as if he already knows the story. The crucial fact that he is his father's killer is revealed by Tiresias, who has summoned Laius's ghost—that is, in Seneca Laius

---

[1] From "An Index of the hardest Words," *Du Bartas His Devine Weekes and Workes Translated* [by Joshua Sylvester] (London, 1613), fol. Iii7ᵛ.

[2] An anonymous 1715 translation of *Oedipus King of Thebes* appears to have been by Lewis Theobald. The publisher Jacob Lintott had commissioned a complete Sophocles translation by Theobald in 1715, but if it was delivered it was never issued; an *Electra* and an *Oedipus King of Thebes* were, however, published anonymously in 1714 and 1715, and reprinted respectively in 1780 and 1765 credited to Theobald. See J. Michael Walton, "Theobald and Lintott: A Footnote on Early Translations of Greek Tragedy," *Arion: A Journal of Humanities and the Classics*, 16.3 (2009), 103–10. For the medieval legend of Gregorius modeled on Oedipus, see Hartmann von Aue, Edwin H. Zeydel, and Bayard Quincy Morgan, *Gregorius: A Medieval Oedipus Legend (The UNC Studies in the Germanic Languages and Literatures*, Vol. 14, Chapel Hill, NC: University of North Carolina Press, 1955); and also Thomas Mann, *The Holy Sinner (Der Erwählte)*, 1951. A complete Sophocles translation by George Adams appeared in 1729, and one by Thomas Francklin in 1758.

posthumously names his killer; by the middle of the play, the fact of Oedipus's guilt is clear and explicit.

The first English *Oedipus* to be based on Sophocles rather than Seneca was John Dryden and Nathaniel Lee's version of 1679, which was both very popular and criticized for being too bloodthirsty. Indeed, although it follows the plot, in the course of adapting Sophocles to the Restoration stage it violates all the classical canons, and not only that of time. It concludes with a number of violent murders committed onstage—including, once, an actual one: At a performance in 1692, the actor playing Creon mistakenly used a real dagger instead of a retractable one, and mortally wounded the actor playing Adrastus. (Dramatically, this was a multiple error: in the play, Adrastus kills Creon, and is himself killed by soldiers.) In fact, Dryden and Lee were no closer to Sophocles than to Seneca.

For the English, in short, Sophocles was an eighteenth- and nineteenth-century dramatist—and, of course, an uncompromisingly modern one. Nevertheless, even to modern eyes *Oedipus* sometimes hit too close to home. When the death of Polybus, whom Oedipus believes to be his father, is revealed, Jocasta says "do not fear that you will wed your mother. Many men before now have slept with their mothers in dreams"[3]—the Oedipus complex for Sophocles was not some deeply buried secret, but common knowledge. Yeats translating the play in 1928, however, omitted the passage—Sophocles was too Freudian for Yeats. The Oedipus story, in fact, has for us required a good deal of interpretation and adaptation; if Yeats found it shocking, modern taste tends to find it uncomfortably tame. The theater impresario Peter Brook, staging Ted Hughes's translation of Seneca's *Oedipus* in 1968, at the play's climax had the cast parade through the audience in the wake of a giant phallus, celebrating Oedipus's expulsion from Thebes by singing "Yes, we have no bananas," accompanied by an energetic jazz band.[4]

---

[3] Lines 980–981 in the Greek text. The translation is by R. C. Jebb.

[4] Ted Hughes did not know Latin, and relied on a prose translation provided to the National Theatre by David Turner, and on the nineteenth-century American translation of Frank Justus Miller published in the Loeb Library Seneca. Hughes was apparently embarrassed by his lack of classical learning, and repeatedly lied about it, but his copy of the Loeb Seneca shows the English translation copiously annotated and not a mark on the Latin text. See Henry Stead, "Seneca's *Oedipus*: By Hook or by Crook," *Canadian Review of Comparative Literature*, 40.1 (March 2013), 88–104.

It was a significant jolt to any expectation of a solemn final catharsis, and thereby an indication of how difficult it is for contemporary culture to take the issues of this classic drama seriously. In the performance I saw, John Gielgud's Oedipus kept forgetting his lines, and had to be prompted constantly—this was, oddly, dramatically effective, emphasizing the tremulousness of Seneca's Oedipus.

Dryden explains the decision to turn for a source to Sophocles rather than Seneca by criticizing Seneca's rhetorical elaboration, "always running after pompous expression, pointed sentences, and Philosophical notions, more proper for the Study than the Stage."[5] This quality, however, was precisely what the sixteenth century (and Roman readers) prized in Seneca. Dryden and Lee duly added to Sophocles what their stage required, not only the concluding blinding and deaths but a good deal of stage business, including two appearances of the ghost of Laius, guilt made manifest, with appropriately ominous effects described in the printed text:

> Peal of Thunder; and flashes of Lightening; then groaning below the stage.[6]

English Classicism

Despite the pervasiveness of the classics in education, the English produced relatively little in the way of classical scholarship during the sixteenth century. The only editions of Greek drama published in England were Euripides's *Trojan Women*, published by John Day in 1575, and Aristophanes's *Knights* published by Joseph Barnes in 1593. In the 1550s Jane, Lady Lumley translated Euripides's *Iphigenia in Aulis* into prose—the translation was apparently done with the assistance of Erasmus's Latin version.[7] It remained unpublished until 1909. George Peele translated one of the *Iphigenia* plays, which was performed by Paul's Boys sometime in the 1570s, and is now lost. The first translation of

---

[5] John Dryden and Nathaniel Lee, *Oedipus: A Tragedy* (London, 1679), Preface, fol. A2ᵛ.
[6] Dryden and Lee, *Oedipus*, p. 38.
[7] See David H. Greene, "Lady Lumley and Greek Tragedy," *The Classical Journal*, 36.9 (June, 1941), 537–47; Alison Findlay, "Reproducing *Iphigenia at Aulis*," *Early Theatre*, 17.2 (2014), 133–201.

a Greek play to be published in English was George Gascoigne and Francis Kinwelmersh's *Jocasta*, a version of Euripides's *Trojan Women*, performed in 1566 and published in Gascoigne's collection *A Hundreth Sundrie Flowres* in 1573. The authors do certainly purport to be translating Euripides—their title reads *Jocasta: A Tragedie writtein in Greke by Euripides. Translated and digested into Acte, by George Gascoigne and Francis Kinwelmersh*—though in fact they are working quite faithfully from a recent Italian version by Lodovico Dolce, which itself is based on a Latin translation. Queen Elizabeth studied Greek with Roger Ascham and was said to have translated a play of Euripides, of which nothing more is known. Considering the prestige of Greek in the educational system the lack of editions may seem surprising, but texts published on the continent were easily available, and presumably English publishers did not anticipate a sufficient market to justify domestic editions.

The works here cited joined a very small number of translations and adaptations of classical drama throughout the sixteenth century in England. Thomas Watson's Latin *Antigone* appeared in 1581; the play had apparently been performed—Gabriel Harvey saw it in London, or perhaps in Cambridge. A Latin edition of Seneca's *Hercules Furens* was published by Henry Sutton in 1561. As for English translations, in 1533 Roger Ascham compiled his *Floures of Latine Spekynge* out of Terence. The Roman dramatist was here treated as a basis not for domestic drama but for Latin conversation—the volume became a standard school text, and was reprinted throughout the century. The interlude *Jack Juggler*, published in 1565, declares itself based on the *Amphitruo* of Plautus; and the other mid-century comedies *Gammer Gurton's Needle* and *Ralph Roister Doister* are similarly modeled on Roman comedy. All ten of the plays attributed to Seneca were published in translation between 1560 and 1581. *Gorboduc*, the most overtly Senecan of sixteenth-century plays in English, is, as we have seen, Senecan only on the page: in performance it was punctuated by long dumb-shows between the acts, and thus to a spectator it would have looked very much like a traditional English tragedy. A translation of Plautus's *Menaechmi* by one "W.W." was issued in 1595 by Thomas Creede, who advertised it as "chosen purposely from out the rest, as least harmefull, and yet most delightfull."[8]

---

[8] For a more detailed account, see my *Wit's Treasury* (Philadelphia: University of Pennsylvania Press, 2021).

Academic drama at the two universities was regularly, though not invariably, performed in Latin, and the public theater troupes were not admitted (therefore the claims of the first quarto of *Hamlet* and of Jonson's *Volpone* to have been played at the universities require some explanation: Were there exceptions? Were the plays performed not at the universities but in the towns, whether in public spaces or at private houses?). Nevertheless, academic drama was informed by the popular stage. Daniel Blank cites a play performed by students at St. John's College, Oxford, in 1602, based on *A Midsummer Night's Dream*, a quarto of which had been published in 1600.[9] And a trilogy of academic plays in English from around 1600, *The Pilgrimage to Parnassus* and its two sequels *The First* and *Second Part of the Returne from Parnassus*, performed by students of St. John's College, Cambridge, concerns a group of scholars taking their degrees at the university and then seeking employment outside of it. In *The Second Part of the Returne from Parnassus* they undertake to become actors, and audition for Richard Burbage and William Kempe, leading performers in the Lord Chamberlain's Men, Shakespeare's company. The actors are depicted as ignorant, and contemptuous of university students. Burbage says, "Few of the university men plaies well, they smell too much of that writer *Ovid*, and that writer *Metamorphoses*, and talke too much of *Proserpina* and *Juppiter*. Why heres our fellow *Shakespeare* puts them all downe."[10] The students for their part complain about having to seek employment in what they consider "the basest trade" of professional acting.[11] Burbage goes on to have one of the students recite the opening lines of Shakespeare's *Richard III*. By the turn of the century, then, Shakespeare was well enough known within the universities to be imitated, satirized, and clearly if ambiguously admired. Gabriel Harvey noted in his copy of Speght's Chaucer (1598) that "The younger sort takes much delight in Shakespeares Venus, & Adonis: but his Lucrece, & his tragedie of

---

[9] *Shakespeare and University Drama in Early Modern England* (Oxford: Oxford University Press, 2023), pp. 1–5.
[10] J. B. Leishman, ed., *The Three Parnassus Plays, 1598–1601* (London: Nicholson and Watson, 1949), 4.3.1766–9.
[11] Leishman, *The Three Parnassus Plays*, 4.4.1846.

Hamlet, Prince of Denmarke, have it in them to please the wiser sort."[12] The note has been dated to 1600–01, before *Hamlet* was in print in any form. The wiser sort were therefore theater audiences as well as readers of poetry.

The Senecan Model

For Renaissance England the key Senecan drama was not *Oedipus*, with its focus on individual guilt, responsibility, and self-knowledge, but *Thyestes*, the tragedy of endless and inexorable revenge. The English taste for revenge drama was especially powerful in the sixteenth and seventeenth centuries; and in fact, one might say that, for the history of theater as its surviving examples allow us to construct it, revenge is the originary subject of drama, and is perhaps the reason drama exists at all. Aeschylus's *Oresteia* trilogy, in showing how society has moved beyond revenge, acknowledged revenge to be a perpetual subject. The final play in the sequence, *The Eumenides*, shows individual revenge being aborted by the gods and judicial punishment reserved to the state (as in the Bible, God forbids individual vengeance, saying "Vengeance is mine"); but this conclusion meant that individual revenge could therefore never be satisfied. One social solution beginning in the Middle Ages was the institutionalization of dueling, a practice that continued almost till modern times despite continued official attempts to suppress it. We may also feel that revenge was endemic in an age when resentment was an inescapable consequence of the political system—indeed, perhaps this is true of any political system: some group always has to lose.

Dryden's pejorative account of the rhetorical character of Senecan drama has been on the whole the predominant one, supported by the assumption that the plays were written not for performance but for declamation. This appears to be the case; the evidence for it is both negative and positive. There are no ancient references to the plays being performed and no Roman actors celebrated for their interpretations of Senecan roles; and the heavily rhetorical nature of the plays themselves

---

[12] Harvey's copy of Speght's Chaucer is now in the British Library, Add. MS 42,518, fol. 422ᵛ. See the detailed discussion by Leo Kirschbaum, "The Date of Shakespeare's 'Hamlet,'" *Studies in Philology*, 34.2 (April, 1937), 168–75.

seems to preclude performance. But as I have argued elsewhere, only the former evidence is really persuasive; the latter reflects only changes in taste, and suggests, on the contrary, that Renaissance performances of Senecan plays were perfectly feasible. James I's favorite play, George Ruggle's *Ignoramus*, presented before him twice at Clare College, Cambridge, has very long speeches in Latin and took six hours to perform. Walter Montagu's *The Shepherd's Paradise*, written for performance by Queen Henrietta Maria and her ladies, had even longer speeches in English. There were complaints about the length from the aristocratic performers, but only the queen's opinion mattered, and the project went ahead. It was eventually performed in a somewhat cut version, but still lasted "seven or eight hours," according to a member of the audience writing after midnight on the night of the event.[13] In both these cases, taste is an issue, but popular taste is not—and if Nero had wanted to see Seneca's plays performed, they would have been performed.[14]

For English readers, T. S. Eliot made Seneca respectable again with two essays, "Seneca in Elizabethan Translation" and "Shakespeare and the Stoicism of Seneca," both published in 1927. These essays on the whole adhere to the traditional view of the heavily rhetorical Seneca, but diverge from it in conceiving Senecan rhetoric a strength, not a weakness. Nevertheless, crucial points depend not on the power of Senecan declamation, but on sudden extremely economical *coups de théâtre*:

> Antony says, "I am Antony still," and the Duchess, "I am Duchess of Malfy still"; would either of them have said that unless Medea had said *Medea superest*? [Medea survives].[15]

Elsewhere Eliot cites the "shock" of Jason's final lines in *Medea*:

> *Per alta vada spatia sublimi aethere,*
> *Testare nullos esse, qua veheris, deos.*[16]
> [Go through the high reaches of thin air,
> Bear witness that where you fly there are no gods.]

---

[13] John Beaulieu to Sir Thomas Puckering, January 10, 1632/3. Thomas Birch, ed., *The Court and Times of Charles the First*, 2 vols (London, 1848), 2: 216.

[14] For the full argument, see *Wit's Treasury*, pp. 129–32.

[15] "Shakespeare and the Stoicism of Seneca," in *Selected Essays of T. S. Eliot* (New York: Harcourt Brace, 1950), p. 113.

[16] "Seneca in Elizabethan Translation," *Selected Essays*, p. 59.

(Or "Bear witness where you fly that there are no gods," the Latin may be construed either way; does the play conclude by denying all religion?) There is, too, the often-quoted response of Thyestes to his brother Atreus, serving Thyestes's murdered sons to him at a bloody banquet:

> Atreus. *Natos ecquid agnoscis tuos?*
> Thyestes.   *Agnosco fratrem.* (1005–1006)
> [*Atreus*. Do you indeed recognize your sons?
> *Thyestes*.   I recognize my brother.]

Arguably, however, the power of these moments depends precisely on their brevity within the surrounding rhetoric. Suddenly the orators are left without words.

Senecan Shakespeare

Early Shakespearean tragedy is imbued with Seneca, as the long rhetorical passages in the *Henry VI* trilogy and in *Richard III* testify. But the most obviously Senecan Shakespeare play is *Titus Andronicus*.[17] The fortunes of this tragedy, indeed, parallel the fortunes of Seneca in the critical literature. In its own time it was one of Shakespeare's most popular plays, the first to be published, in 1594, reissued four times before 1640, translated into Dutch and German and performed on the continent. It is also the only Shakespeare play of which a depiction survives from his lifetime, the Peacham drawing, dating anywhere from 1595 to 1614–15.[18]

The drawing (figure 6.1) gives us a sense of what plays with classical settings looked like on Shakespeare's stage—it cannot be a drawing of a

---

[17] It has been persuasively argued that the play is a collaboration with George Peele. See Macdonald P. Jackson, "Stage Directions and Speech Headings in Act 1 of *Titus Andronicus* Q (1594): Shakespeare or Peele?" *Studies in Bibliography*, 49 (1996), 134–48, and Brian Vickers, *Shakespeare, Co-Author: A Historical Study of Five Collaborative Plays* (Oxford: Oxford University Press, 2002).

[18] See Jonathan Bate's discussion in his edition of *Titus Andronicus*, The Arden Shakespeare, third series (London: Routledge, 1995), pp. 38–43, which concludes that the most likely date is 1614–15. Bate initially resisted the suggestion that the play was a collaboration with Peele, but subsequently concluded that the case was a strong one. See "In the Script Factory," *Times Literary Supplement* (April 15, 2003), 3–4.

FIGURE 6.1   Henry Peacham, drawing based on *Titus Andronicus*, 1595–1614. Longleat, Portland Papers I F. 159v. Reproduced by kind permission of the Marquess of Bath, Longleat House.

performance, since it combines elements from various moments in the play, but it records how a theatergoer of the time imagined the play in action. The drawing gestures toward ancient Rome in the costume of Titus, in the center; but queen Tamora's costume is quite generalized, vaguely medieval, certainly neither Roman nor Elizabethan. Her sons and Aaron the Moor, on the right, are in outfits that combine Elizabethan and Roman elements; the guards on the left are Elizabethan or Jacobean soldiers. The costumes here identify the characters according to their roles and their relation to each other, not to their place in a historical era—there is no attempt here to make the stage a mirror of the Roman world. Within two decades of this drawing, however, Inigo Jones was consulting the best available authorities on ancient Roman dress for his costumes for masques at the court of Charles I. If the king was to be idealized as a classical hero, the classical context had to be authentic.

Titus Andronicus barely survived the closing of the theaters. Edward Ravenscroft, adapting it to the post-restoration stage, declared it "the most incorrect and indigested piece in all [Shakespeare's] works ... rather a heap of Rubbish then a Structure," and considered it unlikely that Shakespeare had in fact written it. Ravenscroft revived it, he said, in the wake of the Popish Plot, to show "the treachery of Villains, and the Mischiefs carry'd on by Perjury, and False Evidence; and how Rogues may frame a Plot that shall deceive and destroy both the Honest and the Wise." In doing so, however, Ravenscroft declared that he had greatly improved the drama: "Compare the Old Play with this, you'l finde that none in all that Authors Works ever receiv'd greater Alterations or Additions, the Language not only refin'd, but many Scenes entirely New: Besides most of the principal Characters heighten'd, and the Plot much encreas'd." The reviser's efforts were duly rewarded: "The Success answer'd the Labour"; despite "the foolish and Malicious part of the Nation ... it bore up against the Faction and is confirm'd a Stock-Play,"[19] that is, one performed regularly (though in fact not often) as part of the acting company's repertoire.

Titus Andronicus has no known source; nevertheless it is a very literary play. At its center is a book. The story of Philomela, Procne, and Tereus in Ovid's *Metamorphoses* is both a model for action and a principle of explanation. The heroine Lavinia, deprived of the power of speech, locates the Philomela story in a copy of Ovid, and names her attackers in writing. The concluding act of revenge, the sons served up to their parents at a banquet, comes directly from Seneca's *Thyestes*. Instead of the Senecan linguistic *coups de théâtre* of the "*Agnosco fratrem*" sort, the play stages a mounting series of outrages—murders, mutilations, severed limbs, beheadings, finally the cannibal banquet. These were not subtle, but they undeniably made for exciting theater. Moreover, the contradictory qualities that for later ages rendered the play unsophisticated were surely for its original audiences high points of the drama: the long, passionate, heavily ornate speeches of Aaron, Tamora, and Titus, and especially Marcus's famous extended ekphrasis upon discovering the mutilated Lavinia:

> Alas, a crimson river of warm blood,
> Like to a bubbling fountain stirred with wind,
> Doth rise and fall between thy rosèd lips ...
>
> (2.3.21ff.)

---

[19] Edward Ravenscroft, *Titus Andronicus, or the Rape of Lavinia* (London, 1687), fol. A2^{r-v}.

For modern readers and directors these speeches are a theatrical problem: What happens onstage during all this rhetoric; what is Lavinia to do while Marcus declaims? The speech continues for almost fifty lines. But surely this is just the sort of thing Shakespeare's audiences came to hear: passionate, ornate oratory. The point is made succinctly by an illustration in G. P. Trapolin's tragedy *Antigone* of 1581 (figure 6.2).

A choral figure stands at the front of the stage addressing the audience—there is no "fourth wall," and despite the perspective setting, no pretense of realism. The motto of the image is a quotation from Seneca's *Thyestes*:

> Let no one trust that good things will follow (i.e., rely on good fortune),
> Let no one despair that better will not come.
>
> (lines 614–15)

Peter Brook's famous production of *Titus Andronicus* in 1957, starring Laurence Olivier and Vivien Leigh, dealt with the theatrical problem simply by cutting Marcus's speech. Jonathan Bate, in the Arden 3 edition of the play, defends the cut by saying that Brook replaced it with some stylized pantomime, but it is clear that Brook simply did not trust the text. Brook also, surely disingenuously, expressed surprise that critics had praised him for saving a bad play, asserting that "it had not occurred to any of us in rehearsal that the play was so bad."[20] Presumably nobody in the company had read any Shakespeare criticism either; Eliot was echoing centuries of critical contempt when he declared *Titus* "one of the stupidest and most uninspired plays ever written, a play in which it is incredible that Shakespeare had any hand at all."[21] Ravenscroft's strictures, cited above, were standard from the late seventeenth century to the mid-twentieth.

The fact that the play is no longer considered bad is surely due in large measure to the success of Brook's production. By 1971, the distinguished classical scholar Reuben Brower could call *Titus Andronicus* "the perfect exhibit of a typical Roman play"[22]—it no longer needed a

---

[20] Bate, *Titus Andronicus*, The Arden Shakespeare, third series, 1.
[21] Eliot, *Selected Essays*, p. 67.
[22] *Hero and Saint: Shakespeare and the Graeco-Roman Heroic Tradition* (New York: Oxford University Press, 1971), p. 173.

FIGURE 6.2 G. P. Trapolin, the Chorus in *Antigone: tragedia* (Padova, 1581), p. 8. Folger Shakespeare Library, 169–641q.

defense. Marcus's ekphrasis, in fact, is profoundly revealing about the nature of Shakespeare's stage. It not only parallels and glosses the action, it effectively pre-empts it:

> But sure some Tereus hath deflowered thee
> And, lest thou shouldst detect him, cut thy tongue.
>
> (2.3.26–7)

Marcus makes the connection with the Tereus/Philomela story immediately. Lavinia later finding the passage in Ovid merely confirms his perception. Language here is both action and interpretation.

Writing in Action

The drama itself is as much writing as action, and in fact, the written word is strikingly emphasized throughout the play. Much of the plotting depends on letters: Aaron's forged letter about Bassianus's death, the letters shot to heaven by Titus's sons, Titus's threatening letter delivered by the clown, even Aaron's extraordinary claim to have dug up corpses and carved on their skins "in Roman letters, 'Let not your sorrow die'" (5.1.140). The Roman letters are there to serve as an eternal reproach specifically to Romans; but the tragic admonition is addressed as well to the literate spectators: English Renaissance education was conducted largely in Latin; moreover, English, of course, is written in Roman letters. Bodies here become texts, just as Lavinia with her tongue cut out is immediately identified as a literary allusion. Demetrius and Chiron knowingly "re-write" the Tereus and Philomela *locus classicus* by cutting off Lavinia's hands as well as her tongue, to prevent her from weaving or embroidering a representation of her rape and mutilation, as Philomela does in *Metamorphoses* VI.

Writing in the play is both action and testimony, and handwriting is always implicitly believed. All Saturninus has to do is show Titus a letter to convince him that his sons are guilty of Bassianus's murder. But letters in Shakespeare are as likely as not to be forged: if handwriting constitutes proof, it also as easily constitutes perjury. What, then, is the real truth of drama? Tamora says that Titus himself found the letter proving his sons' guilt, and he agrees that he did (2.2.294–5); but in fact he did not—this is a case where the character (i.e., the text) lies about action we have seen taking place. The play follows its own rules, and rewrites itself. What, then, is the truth of drama? Aaron's villainy has been self-evident throughout the play, but it only becomes evident to the other characters when a soliloquy of his is overheard—and even this is reported, not dramatized. This is a little epitome of theater: What actors do, after all, is not perform actions but recite lines from scripts. And what audiences know is only what is addressed to them and what they overhear.

Seneca wrote *Thyestes* for an audience that already knew the plot; it turned a familiar narrative into drama. *Titus Andronicus*, a play without a source, constituted a series of unexpected calamities—until, of course, a spectator returned to see it again; for surely its popularity indicates that audiences saw it over and over. Shakespearean drama in this way created its own history.

Taste

Tastes change, and theatrical tastes change rapidly. Jasper Heywood's mid-sixteenth-century translation of *Thyestes*, adapting Latin hexameters to English fourteeners, maintains the verse rhythm rigidly, with no variation for dramatic effect. Here, in modern typography, is Heywood's version of the "*agnosco fratrem*" moment:

> *Thyestes*. . . . Whence murmure they?
> *Atreus*.   With fathers armes embrace them quickely nowe,
> For here they are loe come to thee: dooste thou thy children knowe?
> *Thyestes*. I know my brother: suche a gylt yet canst thou suffre well
> ô earth to beare? nor yet from hence to Stygian lake of hell . . .[23]

The revelation is buried in the metrics. Figure 6.3 shows this moment as it appears in the original edition of 1560. The typography effectively hides the rhetorical *coup*. In Thomas Newton's edition of 1581 (figure 6.4), the regularity of the typography is even more constraining. In contrast, figure 6.5 shows the same moment translated a century later by John Wright, with the drama radically distorting the verse.

[23] *Seneca His Tenne Tragedies, Translated into Englysh* (London, 1581), fol. 37^v.

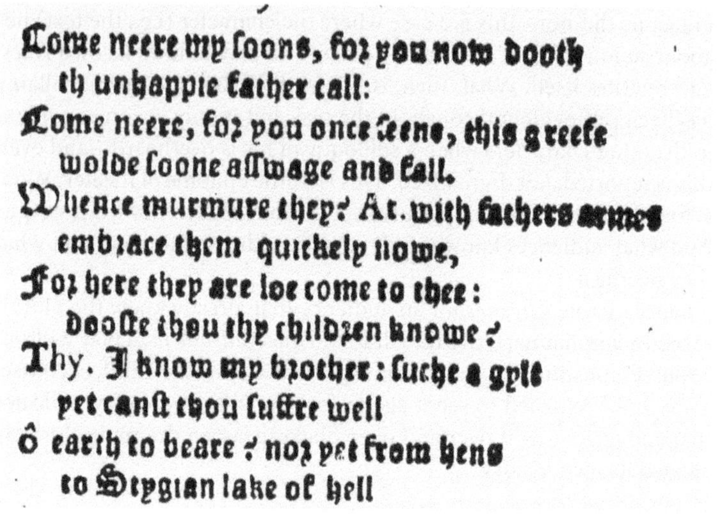

> Come neere my soons, for you now dooth
> th'unhappie father call:
> Come neere, for you once seene, this greefe
> wolde soone asswage and fall.
> Whence murmure they? At. with fathers armes
> embrace them quickely nowe,
> For here they are loe come to thee:
> dooste thou thy children knowe?
> Thy. I know my brother: suche a gylt
> yet canst thou suffre well
> O earth to beare? nor yet from hens
> to Stygian lake of hell

FIGURE 6.3 The seconde tragedie of Seneca entituled Thyestes faithfully Englished by Iasper Heywood (London, 1560), fol. D8ʳ (detail). The Huntington Library, San Marino, CA, 51.961.

> Thiestes
>
> What quakes within? with heauy payse I feele my selfe opprest,
> And with an other voyce then myne bewayles my doleful brest:
> Come nere my sonnes, for you now doth thunhappy father call:
> Come nere, for you once seene, this griefe would soone asswage & fall
> Whence murmure they? A t.w fathers armes embrace them quickly now
> For here they are loe come to thee: dost thou thy children know?
> Th. I know my brother: such a gylt yet canst thou suffer well
> O earth to beare? nor yet from hence to Stygian lake of hell
> Dost thou both drowne thy selfe and vs? nor yet with broaken ground
> Dost thou these kingdomes and their king with Chaos rude confound?

FIGURE 6.4 Seneca His Tenne Tragedies, Translated into Englysh (London, 1581), fol. 37ᵛ (detail).

Thy. What tumult shakes me thus within? My breast
Is with a sad impatient weight oppreft:
Sad groans I with a voice not mine refpire.
Appear my Sons, your moft unhappy fire
Bids you appear: your fight alone will cure
This grief.——Whence anfwer they?
    Atr. ————Make ready your
                      (*Shews the Heads*)
Embraces: they are come,—Now Sir, do ye know
    Your Sons?——
    Atr. I know my Brother.— Canft thou undergo,
Dull earth, fuch wickednefs, & bear it thus?

FIGURE 6.5   J[ohn] W[right], Thyestes A Tragedy, Translated out of Seneca (London, 1684), p. 87.

John Crowne's contemporary play *Thyestes* (1681) is not a translation of Seneca, and therefore is not bound by Seneca's dramaturgy, but, except for an added love-plot between Thyestes's son, here named Philisthenes, and an invented daughter of Atreus named Antigone, it follows Seneca's narrative closely. Crowne's revelation of the murder of Philisthenes (in the play Thyestes has only one son) is conveyed not by rhetoric, but by stage effects, as the father consumes wine mixed with his son's blood:

> Thyestes drinks; a clap of Thunder, the Table oversets, and falls in pieces; all the lights go out.[24]

As for Ravenscroft's *Titus Andronicus*, though the drama is heavily rationalized and the language, as Ravenscroft says, "refined," the climax is nevertheless far more bloodthirsty than Shakespeare's, including, as a backdrop to the banquet, Aaron being tortured on the rack and stubbornly refusing to confess his villainy.

Revenge tragedy was an enormously popular genre partly through satisfying the sadistic tastes of the audience—this was, after all, the same audience for which public executions constituted both a moral spectacle and entertainment—but probably equally because it provided a new kind of protagonist, the hero/villain, the justified murderer. Since as a Christian you believed that murder was never justified and vengeance belonged only to God, Elizabethan revenge plays always have it both ways: they serve as moral sermons on the evils of revenge—the revenger does always lose in the end (though you might say he dies happy)—but audiences have the pleasure of seeing the revenge enacted. The effect is achieved, however, not through the moralizing effects of the drama—nobody in *Titus Andronicus* argues against revenge except Tamora, who is obviously being disingenuous—but through all the action that works against the morality: the thrill of horror at the cunningly planned murders, the actual, physical shock of the violence and its attendant blood, the emotional satisfaction at seeing the villains paid off—these are the most direct effects the plays work with.

---

[24] John Crowne, *Thyestes a Tragedy* (London, 1681), p. 49.

Whole *Hamlets*

In 1589 Thomas Nashe, in his preface to Robert Greene's *Menaphon*, sneered at playwrights who were "a sort of shifting companions, that run through every arte and thrive by none, to leave the trade of *Noverint* [scrivener],[25] whereto they were borne, and busie themselves with the indevors of Art, that could scarcelie latinize their neckeverse if they should have neede"—prisoners condemned to be hanged could save their necks by reading a Latin verse, thus showing that they were literate; but these playwrights were not even that literate in Latin.

Nevertheless, Nashe continues:

> English *Seneca* read by candle light yeeldes manie good sentences, as *Bloud is a begger,* and so foorth: and if you intreate him faire in a frostie morning, he will affoord you whole *Hamlets,* I should say handfulls of tragical speaches.[26]

Uneducated playwrights find plenty of good Senecan effects in translation; and the particular example is *Hamlet*, which Nashe finds especially egregious. There was, then, a *Hamlet* being performed in 1589 that sounded like Seneca—the *Hamlet* familiar to us dates from 1601. The old play must have been popular, since it appears again in the theater manager Philip Henslowe's records as still being performed in 1594. This *Hamlet* was credited to Thomas Kyd because Nashe says its author was born to the trade of *noverint*, scrivener—Kyd's father was a scrivener—and later in the passage says he is one of those who "imitate the Kidde in *Aesop*," suggesting that he is another kid, or Kyd. A case has also been made that it is a very early version of the play by Shakespeare, surviving in some form in the first quarto of *Hamlet*, published in 1603.[27] Nashe's evidence must then be argued away, but Nashe,

---

[25] A scribe, particularly one preparing writs for lawyers. The legal documents prepared by scriveners typically begin "Noverint universi per praesentes . . . ", equivalent to the English formula "Know all men by these presents . . . ", i.e., "Let everyone be informed by this that . . . "

[26] In G. Gregory Smith, ed., *Elizabethan Critical Essays* (Oxford: Oxford University Press, 1904 and many reprints), 1:311–12.

[27] Terri Bourus, *Young Shakespeare's Young Hamlet* (London: Palgrave Macmillan, 2014)—following, notably, Andrew Cairncross, *The Problem of Hamlet: A Solution* (London: Macmillan, 1936)—argues that the first quarto of *Hamlet* is the ur-*Hamlet*, a view

of course, may have been mistaken about the play's authorship. However, the very loose verse of Q1 *Hamlet* sounds nothing like that of early Shakespeare, which is very formal (it also does not sound like Kyd's verse); that may only be because this is a reported text of the sort Thomas Heywood deplores, and Tiffany Stern describes in "Sermons, Plays and Note-Takers" (see above, chapter 1, p. 14).

Nashe's principal charge, however, is of Latin illiteracy. Did Kyd—or Shakespeare—read his Seneca in translation? Many years later Ben Jonson, the most learned of English poets, would write of Shakespeare that he had "small Latin and less Greek"—did Kyd's or Shakespeare's Latin not extend as far as the Seneca studied in school? In that case, their Seneca was the Seneca of Jasper Heywood and the other translators published by Thomas Newton in *Seneca His Tenne Tragedies, Translated into Englysh* in 1581.

Hamlet appears to us more ruminative than declamatory, but that is largely a consequence of our way of performing it. When Hamlet delivers his soliloquies on the modern stage he does so as if he is thinking aloud, speaking only to himself. In the beautiful 1948 film, Laurence Olivier's Hamlet did not even speak the speeches, but remained lost in thought while the soliloquies were recited in a voice-over. But look again at the actor in figure 6.2, the Chorus in a sixteenth-century tragedy: he is at the front of the stage, addressing the audience directly. The Hamlet of 1601 did not think his soliloquies, he declaimed them, arguing, haranguing, justifying himself, persuading the audience of the rightness of his cause and the wickedness of his enemies. Indeed, he accuses himself of overdoing it, "cursing like a very drab." If we think about performing styles, the declamatory Seneca is manifest not merely in the early Shakespeare of *Henry VI* and *Richard III*, but in the tremendous invective of *King Lear* and *Coriolanus*, the passion of *Othello*, both Prospero's rages and his philosophizing.

---

shared by, among others, Harold Bloom, Hardin Craig, and Peter Alexander. See also Steven Urkowitz, "Back to Basics: Thinking about the *Hamlet* First Quarto," in *The Hamlet First Published*, ed. Thomas Clayton (Newark: University of Delaware Press, 1992), pp. 257–91; Alessandro Serpieri, *Il Primo Amleto* (Venice: Marsilio, 1997).

Conclusion

A recurring subject here has been the relation between plays as scripts and plays as books, what it means to conceive of a play as a text, rather than a theatrical event. The other side of this is the extent to which poetry is conceived as performative, whether to be recited aloud to an audience, however small or specific, or to be given as a gift, such as an inscribed manuscript, because the giving of gifts is a performance too. The double question has implications for drama, as when Romeo and Juliet recite sonnets to each other, when the lords in *Love's Labour's Lost* write bad love poetry, or when Orlando tacks poems in praise of Rosalind up on trees. Are Hamlet's soliloquies performative or not? Are they the presentation of a text, or the representation of a man thinking? And alternatively, excerpts from Shakespeare plays begin to get anthologized, as snippets of wisdom or poetic eloquence, very early, by 1599 at least—it is to the point that this happens only after the plays are in print, have become books. Lyric poets like Sidney, Donne, and the Shakespeare of the sonnets make the performative a part of the lyric fiction, so that the poem is in effect one half of a dialogue—"For godsake hold your tongue and let me love," "Farewell, thou art too dear for my possessing."

Returning to the issue of plays as books, Marlowe's *Doctor Faustus*, despite its two printed incarnations, is very much a play even as a book: clearly its transformation into print is incidental; it has only the vaguest sense of an author and seems, in any case, to be a collaboration—if we want it to be Marlowe's greatest play, we nevertheless have a good deal of trouble finding just where Marlowe is in it. We have considered various stages of the play/book relationship, with Shakespeare providing a convenient, if not entirely consistent, set of contrasts between the theatrical quartos and the folio that lives on the library shelf. One epitomizing index to the dramatic implications of the bifurcated life of the play is the use of books and letters on stage: Hamlet's fight with the pirates consists of Horatio reading aloud from a letter about it, as if to insist in the middle of the play that what actors do is not perform actions but recite scripts. In the same way the play as a whole, the memory of Hamlet's story, depends on Horatio's account of it. Can it be merely coincidental that *oratio* is the word for a speech, so that Horatio is an aspirated *oratio*, a living narration? In *Macbeth*, Macbeth's letter to Lady Macbeth about meeting the witches, and their prophecies, is what sets the whole plot of the play in motion. But the letter is a lie, concealing the crucial presence of Banquo in the meeting with the witches, and their prediction about him; and Lady Macbeth's plan of action depends on the lie, as it must do: actors can only perform what is in the script. Dramatic letters often turn out to be not merely lies but outright forgeries: identity depends on handwriting (as we still have to sign documents, like wills and contracts), depends on the fact that the character is the hand (the original meaning of character is a letter of the alphabet; your character is your handwriting), and this means that any character may be impersonated. This becomes one of the commonest of stage conventions, just as nobody ever sees through a disguise in Renaissance drama. The most striking example of the lying letter is in *Twelfth Night*, in Maria's forged letter to Malvolio, which Malvolio recognizes as a love letter from Olivia because he recognizes the handwriting. This is the text he recognizes:

> "To the unknown beloved, this, and my good wishes."

This is what he says about it:

> By my life, this is my lady's hand. These be her very C's, her U's and her T's; and thus she makes her great P's. It is, in contempt of question, her hand.
>
> (2.5.84–8)

Malvolio thus produces this obscene joke. He is being gulled, but far more significantly by Shakespeare than by Maria, because the text he is perusing contains neither C nor P, and handwriting has nothing to do with that. His gloss is impossible; but no Malvolio has ever been able to do anything about it—the character is dependent on the script.

To expand the point, Prospero is dependent on his books for his magic; that is, the action of the play depends on Prospero's books. When he determines to drown his books this is always treated as a renunciation of his magic; but it is even more significantly the character's determination to be free of the script, free of the book of the play. This is what the epilogue demands: Set me free from this play; return me to Milan, but leave the theater and the plot and the book out of it. Jonson represents a critical phase of the development from script to book, the playwright who takes back control of his plays from the actors, revises them for publication and includes a whole range of devices for controlling the response of the readers, as he could never do with audiences.

Every performance of a play differs from every other performance, and every new production of an old play is a new interpretation. That textual instability is obviously not the case when the play becomes a book, though our sense of the play may change as we reread it, and new editions often involve revisions. But also, over the course of history implications and meanings change, and what we require of our classics changes, as does what we consider classics, and as how we present them. For the Greeks and Romans, drama was both a codification of the culture through its legends and mythology and a potent source of entertainment; for many subsequent centuries that vital tradition was ossified into a relatively small corpus of classic drama, whether ignored and discarded as pagan, or deemed useful principally for the study of classical languages.

For the Renaissance, classic drama started as books. The surviving comedies of Terence were published in Strasbourg in 1470, only fifteen years after the beginning of printing in Europe. A collected Plautus was first published in Venice in 1472; the tragedies of Seneca were published in Ferrara in 1484. The surviving corpus of Greek drama was published over two decades by the Aldine Press in Venice, Aristophanes in 1498, Sophocles in 1502, Euripides in 1503, and Aeschylus in 1518. Thus as the Renaissance (the "rebirth" of classical culture) began, classical drama was studied but rarely performed. The first documented post-classical performance of Roman drama, Terence's *Andria*, took place in Florence in 1476; performances of Greek drama began much later.[1] The exquisite Teatro Olimpico in Vicenza, modeled on ancient

---

[1] For an excellent survey, see Francesca Schironi, "The Reception of Ancient Drama in Renaissance Italy," in *A Handbook to the Reception of Greek Drama*, ed. Betine van Zyl Smit (Hoboken, NJ: John Wiley & Sons, 2016), pp. 133–53.

theaters, opened in 1585 with a production of Sophocles' *Oedipus Tyrannos*. The theater had been designed by Andrea Palladio for an academy devoted to the study of classical culture; nevertheless the play was performed not in Greek but in a new Italian translation, which included, moreover, a great deal that was not in the original (the translation is 890 lines longer than the Greek text).[2] Sophocles was inadequate to the Renaissance version of the classics. There were, moreover, no subsequent performances of classical drama in the *Teatro* until modern times. The rebirth in this case was stillborn.

In England for many decades the ancient plays were part of the university curriculum, useful to encourage fluency in Latin and Greek; but even within the academic setting performance could be troubling. John Dee designed a flying machine for a production of Aristophanes' *Peace* in Greek at Trinity College, Cambridge, in 1546. This was a triumph of the science of mechanics, but there were dark mutterings of witchcraft. In 1592 at Christ Church College, Oxford, William Gager's neo-Latin drama *Ulysses Redux* was performed. In it the hero Eurymachus, one of Penelope's suitors, and the servant girl Melantho are lovers; both were of course played by boys, students at the college. John Rainoldes, a Puritan theologian and anti-theatrical polemicist who had survived a long and contentious career at Oxford (and was later one of the translators of the King James Bible) took exception to the behavior of the lovers on stage, charging that they had kissed; this led to an extended debate over the permissability of transvestite theater. Gager plaintively denied that the two boys had kissed, but the issues were much larger, and Rainoldes, a formidable scholar and the stronger debater, is generally held to have had the better of the argument.[3] Here the classics, or perhaps simply the fact of performance itself, was seen as a cover for illicit sexuality.

Though today a small number of Shakespeare plays are performed frequently in various adaptations throughout the world, Shakespeare is institutionalized primarily in books, the multitude of editions: Oxford,

---

[2] The best account is that of Leo Schrade, *La Représentation d'Edipo Tiranno au Teatro Olimpico* (Paris: Centre National de la Recherche Scientifique, 1960).

[3] See John Rainoldes, *Th'overthrow of stage-playes, by the way of controversie betwixt D. Gager and D. Rainoldes ...* (1599); J. W. Binns, "Women or Transvestites on the Elizabethan Stage?: An Oxford Controversy," *The Sixteenth-Century Journal*, 5.2 (October, 1974), 95–120.

Cambridge, Arden, Folger, Pelican, Penguin, Norton, and many others throughout the English-speaking world and in translation. These represent one way of "completing" the plays. Editions, with their introductions, commentary, and apparatus undertake to fill in all the gaps and adjudicate among all the possible alternatives. But in fact, all editions misrepresent the nature of the Shakespearean originals by giving us a single text. For any play on the pre-modern stage, there was not one manuscript, but many, and revision and variation were constant.

But also, all editions, even those which base their texts on a previous edition, differ from one another in a variety of ways, in presentation, commentary, and degree of emendation. Nevertheless, all have shared the assumption that Shakespeare is unreadable—or at least, not marketable—in the original language. Since Nicholas Rowe's edition of 1709, they typically have modernized spelling and punctuation;[4] and though Shakespearean syntax is equally unfamiliar to modern readers, elucidating it is left to the notes, which supply a translation into modern English.

Shakespeare is thus made accessible by being remade in our own image. And yet the England of Shakespeare's time was genuinely different from our world, unfamiliar and even frightening: Witchcraft and the supernatural were treated not simply as poetic fancies but as facts of nature, religion was a pervasive and all too often literally a burning issue, the social hierarchy was everywhere visible and violations of it had real consequences. Shakespeare is now frequently performed in modern dress, which suppresses that difference, though since the characters are invariably still speaking Shakespearean English, the modern dress surely introduces more confusion than familiarity.

Productions set in unfamiliar locales can, of course, be revelatory precisely because they defamiliarize these very familiar texts. Anglophone audiences at Shakespeare productions bring to the theater assumptions and expectations about the plays formed over many years of

---

[4] The major exception is the massive volumes of the New Variorum Shakespeare ("new" because there were several eighteenth-century editions called Variorum), founded by H. H. Furness in 1871, since 1933 sponsored by the Modern Language Association of America, and not yet complete. The Oxford Shakespeare of 1986, edited by Stanley Wells and Gary Taylor, included a single-volume old-spelling edition which, however, is thoroughly modernized in the sense that it makes all the emendations of the modern-spelling edition.

study and familiarity: English speakers grow up with Shakespeare texts. Familiarity can, however, occasion rigidity about texts and inhibit the degree of interpretive innovation possible in performance. In 2015 a London production of *Hamlet* starring Benedict Cumberbatch moved the "To be or not to be" soliloquy to the beginning of the play, to serve as a prologue. This was in fact a thoughtful and even logical decision—the speech makes sense only if it is spoken *before* Hamlet encounters the Ghost, that traveler from the undiscovered country, who tells Hamlet what the speech says we can never know, what happens after death.[5] The *Times*' reviewer was outraged and declared the decision indefensible;[6] the producers, in response, did not attempt a defense, but merely objected to the newspaper reviewing the play while it was still in preview—in subsequent performances the soliloquy was moved, though not to its original place in the third act. This dislocation went unnoticed by the critics. (Thanks to Cumberbatch the production was hugely successful, as it would have been wherever the soliloquy had been placed—the entire run was sold out before the opening.) An energetic debate followed about the legitimacy of reviewing plays at the preview stage, with the *Guardian*'s critic defending the *Times* on the grounds that the theater had not made it clear that the performance was a preview. Throughout, the issue of the validity of the emendation, which had occasioned the initial critical hostility, was not discussed—perhaps deliberately avoided by everyone, as if that were the really dangerous point.

Productions in translation for non-English-speaking audiences, however, present the plays as if new, as, indeed, they are to much of the audience. Such Shakespeare performances are often strikingly original; elements of the plays that to English speakers are over-familiar or seem merely set-pieces can become high points of the drama. The Shakespeare canon is then as unfamiliar as it was to its first audiences. This Shakespeare is the essence of theater, unconstrained by tradition or by

---

[5] Theobald undertook to explain the problem away: "Surely it were easy to say that no traveller returns to this world, as to his home, or abiding place," but ignored the information about the afterlife imparted by the ghost, which Hamlet says we can never know. Coleridge cited the note with approval, but also failed to engage with the crucial part about the afterlife. S. T. Coleridge, *Literary Remains*, ed. H. N. Coleridge (London: Pickering, 1836), p. 2.227.

[6] The review was by Kate Maltby in the issue of August 6, 2015.

prior assumptions. I have seen Italian productions of *Romeo and Juliet* and *Twelfth Night* that were, to someone deeply familiar with the texts, revelations; and yet they did things that, in an Anglophone production, would have been found dubious or even outrageous.

For example, in a production in Rome the title of *Twelfth Night* was completely misinterpreted. The standard Italian translation of the title is *La Dodicesima Notte*, but this is not a correct translation. "Twelfth night" in English refers to Epiphany, the twelfth day of the Christmas season. But "la dodicesima notte," with a direct article, means simply the twelfth in any sequence of nights, not at all limited to the sixth of January. This production interpreted the title as an Arabian Nights story, the twelfth of the thousand and one nights, and therefore gave the play a Middle Eastern setting. This was totally incorrect, but produced a languid, exotic atmosphere that was entirely appropriate for Shakespeare's Illyria. The "Cakes and Ale" scene (2.3), with its rowdy drunkards, often comes across as more painful than funny. Here it was jettisoned, and replaced with a miniature Rossini farce—the music was a pastiche—which allowed Sir Toby, Sir Andrew, Feste, and Maria to produce a thrilling comic energy that had the audience cheering at its conclusion. Malvolio's interruption, which can come as a relief in performances of the original text, was here the disappointment that it must have been on Shakespeare's stage. This editorial and directorial stratagem would doubtless have produced indignation on an Anglophone stage; in Rome it seemed entirely justified, and established the comic characters as genuinely funny.[7] In fact, as we have seen, the difference between the performing tradition and the textual tradition has been very large for several centuries—judging from Jonson's assertion that the quarto of *Every Man Out of His Humour* includes "more than hath been Publickely Spoken or Acted" and Humphrey Moseley's claim to deliver in his Beaumont and Fletcher edition "All that was *Acted*, and all that was not," it dates from Shakespeare's own time.

---

[7] For a fuller account of the two productions, see my essay "Shakespeare all'italiana," in my collection *The Invention of Shakespeare and Other Essays* (Philadelphia: University of Pennsylvania Press, 2022), pp. 151–9.

In short, we miss a great deal when we ignore the transformations from event to text to event. Paul Menzer's learned and witty *Anecdotal Shakespeare* is precisely about how much our sense of Shakespeare depends not upon texts, but upon the effects and recollections—frequently transmuted or even invented—of individual performances.[8]

The Apotheosis of the Book: The Cranach Press *Hamlet*

Hamlet has always had a special place in the Shakespeare canon. In Shakespeare's own time Gabriel Harvey said that "the wiser sort" admired it, and two centuries later Coleridge, indignant at eighteenth-century critics finding fault with the play (as Johnson had called it seriously implausible), declared it Shakespeare's deepest expression of himself.[9] The play was refigured through an idea of comprehensiveness into the most monumental book of the twentieth century. The Cranach Press *Hamlet* was published in a German edition in 1929 and in an English edition in 1930.[10] For this tremendously ambitious project, the publisher Count Harry Kessler commissioned a new type based on a font used in one of the earliest books printed in Germany, the magnificent Mainz Psalter of 1457. The artist and theater designer Edward Gordon Craig, son of the great actress Ellen Terry, was engaged to produce illustrative woodcuts, and the book was printed with hand presses on handmade paper in limited editions of 230 copies for the German version, 300 for the English.

Craig had started as an actor; in 1894 and 1896 in Henry Irving's company he had played Hamlet—his mother had played Ophelia to Irving's Hamlet in 1878–79. In 1911, as a stage designer, he collaborated with Konstantin Stanislavski on a *Hamlet* for the Moscow Art Theater.

---

[8] *Anecdotal Shakespeare: A New Performance History* (London: Bloomsbury Arden Shakespeare, 2015).

[9] Lecture on *Hamlet*, January 12, 1812, in J. P. Collier, ed., *Samuel Taylor Coleridge, Seven Lectures on Shakespeare and Milton* (London: Chapman and Hall, 1856), pp. 141–9.

[10] *Die tragische Geschichte von Hamlet, Prinzen von Dænemark* (Weimar: Cranach Presse, 1929); J. Dover Wilson, ed., *The Tragedie of Hamlet, Prince of Denmarke* (Weimar: Cranach Press, 1930). This account of the book is adapted from my essay "The Desire and Pursuit of the Whole," in *The Invention of Shakespeare and Other Essays*, pp. 23–33.

For this he designed a non-realistic stage the central element of which was a set of complex, moveable screens. The collaboration was, from the outset, not a success. Craig's abstract theater was the wrong setting for Stanislavski's intensely psychologized, character-centered, view of drama; moreover, the screens could not be got to work properly, and kept falling down. But the concept remained with Craig, and the stage he could not create for Stanislavski he realized on the page for Kessler.

Kessler's idea was to present *Hamlet* in a Renaissance setting. The book would be a reflection of what he conceived as the historical *Hamlet*—not the *Hamlet* of the quartos, or the Shakespeare folio, and least of all any putative "real" Hamlet, but a bibliographic embodiment of the towering monument to Renaissance culture that *Hamlet* had become. It would complete the *idea* of *Hamlet*. So the models for the book were the masterpieces of the great fifteenth- and sixteenth-century European presses. Kessler's type face was thus based not on a font from Shakespeare's age, but on the grandest of the early German models: this Hamlet was the German intellectual, the student at the University of Wittenburg, the humanist philosopher and scholar. The design of the book was that of a very grand late fifteenth- or early sixteenth-century scholarly edition: the text was in the center of the page, and in the margins around it, in smaller type, related material was placed.

In sixteenth-century editions, the marginal material would have consisted of commentary and notes; Kessler's marginalia were the play's main sources, the Hamlet story in the Latin chronicle of Saxo Grammaticus and the French *Histoires Tragiques* of François de Belleforest. These were printed in both the original languages and in translation. For the German edition, the text was the standard translation of Friedrich Schlegel, embellished by the modern poet Gerhardt Hauptmann, who supplied several additional (and rather pointless) scenes, such as the reception of Claudius's emissaries Voltimand and Cornelius by the Norwegian king, to fill in what he conceived to be gaps in the plot, and thereby render the play more "complete" than the original. (Hauptmann's version of Schlegel's translation itself was not unproblematic: for example, it moves the "To be or not to be" soliloquy to the fifth act—to my knowledge, no German critic ever objected.) For the English edition, the Shakespearean scholar J. Dover Wilson prepared a more straightforward text preserving the original spelling and based on the second quarto—not, significantly, a conflation of the quarto and folio, which regularly constituted the "complete" English text in the period.

Craig provided seventy-two woodcuts for the German edition, and five additional ones for the English version. The deployment of these on the page resembles more the format of a Renaissance book than any illustrated scholarly Shakespeare: the images are not contained by the typography, but are in a full partnership with it, and sometimes seem even in control.[11] Hamlet and Horatio await the ghost, dwarfed by a setting composed of a combination of Craig's woodcut screens, Shakespeare's text, and Saxo's chronicle. Throughout the book, Craig's images are beautifully attuned to the play's changes of mood. Several of the woodcuts were printed in two stages, to register lighter and darker blacks. For the Play Scene, a cast of *commedia dell'arte* characters in black silhouette appears in various formats—free-standing across the bottom margin, within whole scenes incised with white on black and grey backgrounds, in a tiny roundel in the center of a page, and most startling, for the Dumb Show, two elaborately masked and costumed silhouettes replacing the central text on two facing pages, with the description of the pantomime printed in red beneath them. Ophelia's last appearance is as a tiny white waiflike form within a grid of pale blue flanked by two of Craig's massive black woodcut screens, with a silhouetted mob beyond them—this is the only use of color in the woodcuts, and it is tremendously affecting.

There is no illustrated Shakespeare in which the images are so thoroughly integrated with the typography, and in which text, book, and performance are conceived so completely as a whole. The Cranach Press *Hamlet* undertakes to rethink the relation of drama, book, and image—in short, the nature of dramatic representation on the page—from the beginning; reconceives the book of the play as a performance, and completes the play as a book.

---

[11] My original intention was to include illustrations from the book. But repeated attempts over more than a month to communicate with the copyright owner, the Edward Gordon Craig Estate, went unanswered. Two pages are reproduced in my essay "The Desire and Pursuit of the Whole," in my collection *The Invention of Shakespeare and Other Essays* (University of Pennsylvania Press, 2022)—the Craig Estate was admirably responsive two years ago—and the Folger Shakespeare Library has digitized several pages at https://luna.folger.edu/luna/servlet/detail/FOLGERCM1~6~6~1235917~236120:-Hamlet—German—1928—Die-tragisch?qvq=q:edward%20gordon%20craig&mi=9&trs=10

PRINCIPAL WORKS DISCUSSED

Beaumont, Francis, and John Fletcher, *Comedies and Tragedies Written by Francis Beaumont and John Fletcher*, 1647.
Harington, Sir John, masque of Solomon and the Queen of Sheba, 1606; account first published 1775.
Jonson, Ben, *Works*, 1616, 1640–41.
Kyd, Thomas, *The Spanish Tragedie*. Performed before 1588; published 1592.
Medwall, Henry, *Fulgens and Lucres*. Performed c.1497, published c.1512.
Marlowe, Christopher, *Tamburlaine the Great*, c.1588, published 1590.
Middleton, Thomas, *A Game at Chesse*. Performed 1624; published c.1625 (three undated editions) and in several manuscripts, both holograph and scribal.
Moseley, Humphrey, "The Stationer to the Reader," prefatory epistle to *Comedies and Tragedies Written by Francis Beaumont and John Fletcher*. 1647.
Norton, Thomas, and Thomas Sackville, *The Tragedie of Gorboduc*. Performed 1560–61; published in a revised edition by William Griffiths, 1565. New edition published by John Day, 1570, under the title *The Tragidie of Ferrex and Porrex*. Third edition under the title *The Tragedye of Gorboduc* appended to John Lydgate's *The Serpent of Devision*, 1590.
Seneca, *Oedipus*, trans. Ted Hughes. Performed 1968; published 1983.
Seneca, *Thyestes*, trans. Jasper Heywood. 1560; trans. John Crowne, 1681.
Seneca, *Seneca His Tenne Tragedies, Translated into Englysh*, ed. Thomas Newton 1581.
Shakespeare, William, *Die tragische Geschichte von Hamlet, Prinzen von Dænemark* (Weimar: Cranach Presse, 1929); J. Dover Wilson, ed., *The Tragedie of Hamlet, Prince of Denmarke* (Weimar: Cranach Press, 1930).
Shakespeare, William, *Macbeth* 1623 (first folio); as adapted by Sir William Davenant, *Macbeth a tragedy: with all the alterations, amendments, additions, and new songs*. 1674.
Shakespeare, William, *Romeo and Juliet*, 1597 (first quarto), 1599 (second quarto), 1623 (first folio).
Shakespeare, William, *The Tempest* (first folio, 1623); as adapted by Davenant and John Dryden, *The Tempest, or The enchanted island, a comedy* 1674.
Shakespeare, William, *Titus Andronicus* 1594; as adapted by Edward Ravenscroft 1687.
Shakespeare, William, *Comedies, Histories, and Tragedies*, 1623 (first folio), 1632 (second folio), 1663 (third folio), 1664 (third folio, second issue, with seven additional plays), 1685 (fourth folio, including the additional plays); ed.

Nicholas Rowe (plays) and Charles Gildon (poems), 7 vols (1709–10); ed. Alexander Pope, 6 vols (1723–25); revised edition, 8 vols (1728); ed. Lewis Theobald (1734); ed. Samuel Johnson (1765).

Sophocles, *Oedipus Tyrannos*, trans. John Dryden and Nathaniel Lee. 1679.

Sophocles, trans. W. B. Yeats. 1928.

Theobald, Lewis, *Shakespeare Restored, or a Specimen of the many Errors as well Committed as Unamended by Mr Pope in his late edition of this poet*. 1726.

BIBLIOGRAPHY

Primary Sources

Anon., *Wits Recreations* (1640).
Beaumont, Francis, and John Fletcher, *Comedies and Tragedies Written by Francis Beaumont and John Fletcher* (London, 1647).
Campion, Thomas, *The discription of a maske, presented before the Kinges Maiestie at White-Hall, on Twelfth Night last in honour of the Lord Hayes, and his bride ...* (*Lord Hay's Masque*) (1607).
Chamberlain, John, *Letters of John Chamberlain*, ed. Norman E. McClure (2 vols, Philadelphia: American Philosophical Society, 1939).
Crowne, John, *Thyestes a Tragedy* (London, 1681).
Daniel, Samuel, *Cleopatra* (1594).
Daniel, Samuel, *Works* (1601).
Davenant, Sir William, and John Dryden, *The Tempest, or the Enchanted Island* (1670).
Dryden, John, and Nathaniel Lee, *Oedipus: A Tragedy* (London, 1679).
Du Bartas, Sylvester, *Du Bartas His Devine Weekes and Workes Translated* (London, 1613).
Forman, Simon, *The Bocke of Plaies and Notes therof per Forman for Common Pollicie*, Bodleian Library (MS Ashmole 208), accessible at https://shakespearedocumented.folger.edu/resource/document/formans-account-seeing-plays-globe-macbeth-cymbeline-winters-tale.
Gager, William, *Ulysses Redux* (1591).
Gascoigne, George, and Francis Kinwelmarsh, *Jocasta* (perf. 1566, pub. 1573).
Greene, Robert (?), *Greene's Groatsworth of Wit* (1592).
Harington, Henry, *Nugae Antiquae* (2 vols, London, 1769–75).
Herbert, Mary Sidney, Countess of Pembroke, *Antonie* (1593); *Antonius* (1595).
Heywood, Thomas, *An Apology for Actors* (1612).
Heywood, Thomas, *The Brazen Age* (1613).
Heywood, Thomas, *The Rape of Lucrece* (1608).
James I, *Basilicon Doron* (1603).
James I, *Daemonology* (1597).
Jonson, Ben, *The Alchemist* (1612).
Jonson, Ben, *Catiline* (1611, 1635).
Jonson, Ben, *Chloridia* (1631).

Jonson, Ben, *Every Man Out of His Humour* (1600).
Jonson, Ben, *Hymenaei* (1606).
Jonson, Ben, *Love's Triumph Through Callipolis* (1631).
Jonson, Ben, *The New Inn* (1631).
Jonson, Ben, *Volpone* (1607).
Jonson, Ben, *Workes* (1616, 1640–41).
Jonson, Ben, *The Cambridge Edition of the Works of Ben Jonson*, ed. David Bevington, Martin Butler, and Ian Donaldson (7 vols, Cambridge: Cambridge University Press, 2012).
Kyd, Thomas, *Cornelia* (1595).
Kyd, Thomas, *Soliman and Perseda* (1592).
Kyd, Thomas, *The Spanish Tragedy* (1592).
Kyd, Thomas, *The Spanish Tragedy*, ed. Clara Calvo and Jesus Tronch (*Arden Early Modern Drama*, London: Bloomsbury, 2013).
Leishman, J. B., ed., *The Three Parnassus Plays, 1598–1601* (London: Nicholson and Watson, 1949).
Lumley, Jane, Lady, *Iphigenia in Aulis* (London: The Malone Society, 1909).
Marlowe, Christopher, *Tamburlaine* (1590).
Marston, John, *The Workes ... being Tragedies and Comedies* (1633).
Medwall, Henry, *Fulgens and Lucres* (c.1511).
Middleton, Thomas, *A Game at Chesse*, Bridgewater Manuscript, EL34 B17 Huntington Library, San Marino, CA.
Middleton, Thomas, Trinity College, Cambridge Manuscript, O.2.66, Wren digital library.
Middleton, Thomas, Folger Shakespeare Library Manuscript V.a.231(61).
Middleton, Thomas, *A Game at Chess*, ed. R. C. Bald (Cambridge: Cambridge University Press, 1929).
Middleton, Thomas, *A Game at Chess*, ed. M. A. Buettner (Lewiston, NY: Edwin Mellen Press, 1980).
Middleton, Thomas, *Thomas Middleton: The Collected Works*, ed. Gary Taylor and John Lavagnino (Oxford: Clarendon Press, 2007).
Middleton, Thomas, *The Witch* (1778).
Nashe, Thomas, *Pierce Penilesse His Supplication to the Divell* (1592).
Norton, Thomas, and Thomas Sackville, *Gorboduc* (1565).
Overbury, Sir Thomas, *The Wife* (1614).
Rainoldes, John, *Th'overthrow of stage-playes, by the way of controversie betwixt D. Gager and D. Rainoldes ...* (1599).
Ravenscroft, Edward, *Titus Andronicus, or the Rape of Lavinia* (London, 1687).
Seneca, *Tragedies*, trans. John G. Hitch, vol. 2 (Loeb Classical Library, Cambridge, MA: Harvard University Press, 2018).
Seneca, *Seneca His Tenne Tragedies, Translated into Englysh*, ed. Thomas Newton (London, 1581).

Seneca, *Oedipus*, adapted by Ted Hughes (London: Faber and Faber, 1969).
Shakespeare, William, *Hamlet* (1603) (Q1).
Shakespeare, William, *Hamlet*(1605) (Q2).
Shakespeare, William, *Macbeth* (1623).
Shakespeare, William, *The New Oxford Shakespeare*, ed. Gary Taylor et al. (Oxford: Oxford University Press, 2016).
Shakespeare, William, *The Oxford Shakespeare*, ed. Stanley Wells and Gary Taylor (Oxford: Oxford University Press, 1986).
Shakespeare, William, *Julius Caesar*, ed. *Arthur Humphreys* (Oxford: Oxford University Press, 1984).
Shakespeare, William, *Romeo and Juliet* (1597).
Shakespeare, William, *Romeo and Juliet* (1599).
Shakespeare, William, *The Tempest*, ed. Frank Kermode (The Arden Shakespeare series 2, revised edition, London: Methuen, 1954).
Shakespeare, William, *Titus Andronicus*, ed. Jonathan Bate (Arden Shakespeare, series 3, London: Routledge 1995).
Shakespeare, William, *The Tragedie of Hamlet, Prince of Denmarke*, ed. J. Dover Wilson (Weimar: Cranach Press, 1930).
Shakespeare, William, *Die tragische Geschichte von Hamlet, Prinzen von Dænemark* (Weimar: Cranach Presse, 1929).
Shakespeare, William, *Troilus and Cressida* (1609).
Shakespeare, William, *The Tempest*, ed. Stephen Orgel (The Oxford Shakespeare, Oxford: Clarendon Press, 1987).
Shakespeare, William, *The Tempest*, ed. Virginia Mason Vaughan and Alden T. Vaughan (Arden Shakespeare series 3, revised edition, London: Bloomsbury 2011).
Shakespeare, William, *The Works of Mr. William Shakespear*, ed. Nicholas Rowe, 7 vols (London, 1709–10).
Shakespeare, William, et. al., *The Passionate Pilgrim* (1599).
Sophocles, *Oedipus Tyrannos, The Tragedies of Sophocles from the Greek*, trans. Thomas Francklin (London, 1758).
Sophocles, Yeats as *King Oedipus*, trans. W. B. Yeats (London: Macmillan, 1928).
Sophocles, *Electra*, trans. Charles Wase (1649).

Secondary Sources

Agnew, Jean-Christophe, *Worlds Apart: The Market and the Theater in Anglo-American Thought, 1550–1750* (Cambridge: Cambridge University Press, 1986).
Barish, Jonas, *The Anti-Theatrical Prejudice* (Berkeley: University of California Press, 1981).

Barton, Anne (Anne Righter), *Ben Jonson, Dramatist* (Cambridge: Cambridge University Press, 1984).
Bate, Jonathan, "In the Script Factory," *Times Literary Supplement* (April 15, 2003), 3–4.
Berger, Harry, Jr., "The Early Scenes of Macbeth : Preface to a New Interpretation," in *Making Trifles of Terrors*, ed. Harry Berger, Jr. (Stanford: Stanford University Press, 1997), pp. 70–97.
Berger, Harry, Jr., *Imaginary Audition: Shakespeare on Stage and Page* (Berkeley: University of California Press, 1989).
Bevington, David, and Peter Holbrook eds, *The Politics of the Stuart Court Masque* (Cambridge: Cambridge University Press, 1998).
Binns, J. W., "Women or Transvestites on the Elizabethan Stage?: An Oxford Controversy," *The Sixteenth-Century Journal*, 5.2 (October, 1974), 95–120.
Birch, Thomas, ed., *The Court and Times of Charles the First*, 2 vols (London, 1848).
Blank, Daniel, *Shakespeare and University Drama in Early Modern England* (Oxford: Oxford University Press, 2023).
Blayney, Peter, "The Publication of Playbooks," in *A New History of Early English Drama*, ed. John D. Cox and David Scott Kastan (New York: Columbia University Press, 1997), pp. 383–422.
Bourne, Claire, *Typographies of Performance in Early Modern England* (Oxford: Oxford University Press, 2020).
Bourus, Terri, *Young Shakespeare's Young Hamlet* (London: Palgrave Macmillan, 2014).
Brooks, Douglas, *From Playhouse to Printing House* (Cambridge: Cambridge University Press, 2000).
Brower, Reuben, *Hero and Saint: Shakespeare and the Graeco-Roman Heroic Tradition* (New York: Oxford University Press, 1971).
Bruster, Douglas, "Shakespearean Spellings and Handwriting in the Additional Passages Printed in the 1602 *Spanish Tragedy*," *Notes and Queries*, 60 (2013), 420–4.
Butler, Martin, *The Stuart Court Masque and Political Culture* (Cambridge: Cambridge University Press, 2008).
Butler, Martin, "'We are one mans all': Jonson's 'The Gipsies Metamorphosed,'" *The Yearbook of English Studies*, 21 (1991), 253–73.
Cairncross, Andrew, *The Problem of Hamlet: A Solution* (London: Macmillan, 1936).
Chartier, Roger, *Publishing Drama in Early Modern Europe* (The Panizzi Lectures, London: The British Library, 1998).
Coleridge, Samuel Taylor, *Seven Lectures on Shakespeare and Milton* ed. J. P. Collier (London: Chapman and Hall, 1856).

Coleridge, Samuel Taylor, *Literary Remains*, ed. H. N. Coleridge (London: Pickering, 1836).

Cormack, Bradin, "Shakespeare's Narcissus, Sonnet's Echo," in *The Forms of Renaissance Thought*, ed. Leonard Barkan, Bradin Cormack, and Sean Keilen (Houndsmill: Palgrave Macmillan, 2009).

De Grazia, Margreta, and Peter Stallybrass, "The Materiality of the Shakespearean Text," *Shakespeare Quarterly* 44 (1993), 255–83.

Dennis, John, "On the Genius and Writings of Shakespear," letter 3, in *Eighteenth-Century Essays on Shakespeare*, ed. D. Nichol Smith (2nd edition, Oxford: Oxford University Press, 1963), pp. 39–42.

Dobson, Michael, *The Making of the National Poet* (Oxford: Clarendon Press, 1992).

Duthie, G. I., "The Text of Shakespeare's *Romeo and Juliet*," *Studies in Bibliography*, 4 (1951/1952), 3–29.

Dutton, Richard, *Shakespeare, Court Dramatist* (Oxford: Oxford University Press, 2016).

Eliot, T. S., "Seneca in Elizabethan Translation," in *Selected Essays of T. S. Eliot* (New York: Harcourt Brace, 1950).

Eliot, T. S., "Shakespeare and the Stoicism of Seneca," in *Selected Essays of T. S. Eliot* (New York: Harcourt Brace, 1950).

Erne, Lukas, *Beyond The Spanish Tragedy* (Revels Plays Companion Library, Manchester: Manchester University Press, 1988).

Erne, Lukas, ed., *The First Quarto of Romeo and Juliet* (Cambridge: Cambridge University Press, 2007).

Erne, Lukas, *Shakespeare and the Book Trade* (Cambridge: Cambridge University Press, 2013).

Evans, G. Blakemore, ed., *Shakespearean Prompt-Books of the Seventeenth Century*, Vol. I: *The Padua "Macbeth"* (Charlottesville: University of Virginia Press, 1960); Vol. II, *The Padua "Measure for Measure"* (1963).

Farmer, Alan B., and Zachary Lesser, "The Popularity of Playbooks Revisited," *Shakespeare Quarterly*, 56.1 (2005), 1–32.

Findlay, Alison, "Reproducing *Iphigenia at Aulis*," *Early Theatre* 17.2 (2014), 133–201.

Franko, Mark, *Dance as Text: Ideologies of the Baroque Body* (revised edition, Oxford: Oxford University Press, 2015).

Goldberg, Jonathan, "'What? in a names that which we call a Rose,' The Desired Texts of *Romeo and Juliet*," in *Crisis in Editing: Texts of the English Renaissance*, ed. Randall Mcleod (New York: AMS Press, 1994), pp. 173–202.

Greenblatt, Stephen, *Will in the World* (New York: W. W. Norton, 2004).

Greene, David H., "Lady Lumley and Greek Tragedy," *The Classical Journal*, 36.9 (June 1941), 537–47.

Ingleby, C. M. et al., *The Shakespere Allusion Book* (new edition, London: Oxford University Press, 1932).

Jackson, Macdonald P., "Stage Directions and Speech Headings in Act 1 of *Titus Andronicus* Q (1594): Shakespeare or Peele?" *Studies in Bibliography*, 49 (1996), 134–48.

James, Henry, and Greg Walker, "The Politics of *Gorboduc*," *English Historical Review* 110. 435 (February 1995), 109–21.

Kastan, David, "The Mechanics of Culture: Editing Shakespeare Today," *Shakespeare Studies* 24 (1996), 30–7.

Kirschbaum, Leo, "The Date of Shakespeare's 'Hamlet,'" *Studies in Philology*, 34.2 (April 1937), 168–75.

Lesser, Zachary, *Renaissance Drama and the Politics of Publication: Readings in the English Book Trade* (Cambridge: Cambridge University Press, 2004).

Lesser, Zachary, and Peter Stallybrass, "The First Literary *Hamlet* and the Commonplacing of Professional Plays," *Shakespeare Quarterly*, 59.4 (2008), 371–420.

McInnis, David, and Matthew Steggle, eds, *Lost Plays in Shakespeare's England* (Houndsmill: Palgrave Macmillan, 2014).

Mann, Thomas, *The Holy Sinner (Der Erwählte)*, trans. H. T. Lowe-Porter (New York: Knopf, 1951).

Marcus, Leah S., *Unediting the Renaissance: Shakespeare, Marlowe, Milton* (London: Routledge, 1996).

Marino, James J., *Owning William Shakespeare* (Philadelphia: University of Pennsylvania Press, 2011).

Menzer, Paul, *Anecdotal Shakespeare: A New Performance History* (London: Bloomsbury Arden Shakespeare, 2015).

Menzer, Paul, *The* Hamlets: *Cues, Qs, and Remembered Texts* (Newark, DE: University of Delaware Press, 2008).

Mowat, Barbara, "The Problem of Shakespeare's Text(s)," in *Textual Formations and Reformations*, ed. Laurie Maguire and Thomas Berger (Newark, DE: University of Delaware Press, 1998), pp. 131–48.

Nichols, John, *The Progresses, Processions, and Magnificent Festivities, of King James the First* (London, 1828).

Orgel, Stephen, "Acting Scripts, Performing Texts," in Stephen Orgel, *The Authentic Shakespeare* (New York: Routledge, 2022), 21–48.

Orgel, Stephen, *The Idea of the Book and the Creation of Literature* (Oxford: Oxford University Press, 2023).

Orgel, Stephen, *Inigo Jones* (London and Berkeley: Sotheby and University of California Press, 1973).

Orgel, Stephen, *The Invention of Shakespeare and Other Essays* (Philadelphia: University of Pennsylvania Press, 2022).

Orgel, Stephen, *The Reader in the Book: A Study of Spaces and Traces* (Oxford: Oxford University Press, 2015).

Orgel, Stephen, *Wit's Treasury: Renaissance England and the Classics* (Philadelphia: University of Pennsylvania Press, 2021).

Preiss, Richard, *Clowning and Authorship in Early Modern Theatre* (Cambridge: Cambridge University Press, 2014).

Prosdocimi, Lavinia, "Un fondo appartenuto alla *natio Anglica*. Il *First Folio* e altri libri inglesi della Biblioteca universitaria," in *Intellettuali e Uomini di Corte*, ed. Ester Pietrobon (Roma: Donzelli Editore, 2021), pp. 205–16.

Randall, Dale B. J., *Jonson's Gypsies Unmasked* (Durham, NC: Duke University Press, 1975).

Riggs, David, *Ben Jonson* (Cambridge, MA: Harvard University Press, 1989).

Ravelhofer, Barbara, *The Early Stuart Masque: Dance, Costume, and Music* (Oxford: Oxford University Press, 2006).

Sabol, Andrew, *Four Hundred Songs and Dances from the Stuart Masque* (Providence: Brown University Press, 1977).

Schoch, Richard, and Amanda Eubanks Winkler, *Shakespeare in the Theatre: Sir William Davenant and the Duke's Company* (The Arden Shakespeare, London: Bloomsbury, 2022).

Schrade, Leo, *La Représentation d'Edipo Tiranno au Teatro Olimpico* (Paris: Centre National de la Recherche Scientifique, 1960).

Schironi, Francesca, "The Reception of Ancient Drama in Renaissance Italy," in *A Handbook to the Reception of Greek Drama*, ed. Betine van Zyl Smit (Hoboken, NJ: John Wiley & Sons, 2016), pp. 133–53.

Serpieri, Alessandro, *Il Primo Amleto* (Venice: Marsilio, 1997).

Smith, G. Gregory, ed., *Elizabethan Critical Essays* (Oxford: Oxford University Press, 1904).

Speaight, Robert, *William Poel and the Elizabethan Revival* (Cambridge, MA: Harvard University Press, 1954).

Stead, Henry, "Seneca's Oedipus: By Hook or by Crook," *Canadian Review of Comparative Literature*, 40.1 (March 2013), 88–104.

Stern, Tiffany, *Making Shakespeare: From Stage to Page* (London: Routledge, 2004).

Stern, Tiffany, "Plays in the Stationers' Register in the Time of Shakespeare" (2017). Web publication/site, Adam Matthew. http://www.literaryprintculture.amdigital.co.uk.

Stern, Tiffany, "Sermons, Plays and Note-Takers: Hamlet Q1 as a 'Noted' Text," *Shakespeare Survey*, 66 (2013), 1–23.

Stern, Tiffany, "Time for Shakespeare: Hourglasses, Sundials, Clocks, and Early Modern Theatre," *Journal of the British Academy*, 3 (2015), 1–33.

Straznicky, Marta, ed., *The Book of the Play* (Amherst: University of Massachussets Press, 2006).

Suthren, Carla, "Translating Commonplacing Marks in Gascoigne and Kinwelmersh's *Jocasta*," *Translation and Literature*, 29.1 (March 2020), 59–84.

Thomas, Max W., "Eschewing Credit: Heywood, Shakespeare, and Plagiarism before Copyright," *New Literary History*, 31.2 (Spring, 2000), 277–93.

Urkowitz, Steven, "Back to Basics: Thinking about the Hamlet First Quarto," in *The Hamlet First Published*, ed. Thomas Clayton (Newark: University of Delaware Press, 1992), pp. 257–91.

Vickers, Brian, "Identifying Shakespeare's Additions to *The Spanish Tragedy* (1602): A New(er) Approach," *Shakespeare*, 8.1 (2012), 13–43.

Vickers, Brian, *Shakespeare, Co-Author: A Historical Study of Five Collaborative Plays* (Oxford: Oxford University Press, 2002).

von Aue, Hartmann, *Gregorius: A Medieval Oedipus Legend*, ed. Edwin H. Zeydel and Bayard Quincy Morgan (The UNC Studies in the Germanic Languages and Literatures, Vol. 14, Chapel Hill, NC: University of North Carolina Press, 1955).

Walton, J. Michael, "Theobald and Lintott: A Footnote on Early Translations of Greek Tragedy," *Arion: A Journal of Humanities and the Classics*, 16.3 (2009), 103–10.

Weimann, Robert, *Author's Pen and Actor's Voice* (Cambridge: Cambridge University Press, 2000).

Werstine, Paul, "A Century of 'Bad' Shakespeare Quartos," *Shakespeare Quarterly*, 50.3 (1999), 310–33.

Werstine, Paul, "Shakespeare, More or Less: A. W. Pollard and Twentieth-Century Shakespeare Editing," *Florilegium*, 16 (1999), 25–45.

Williams, George Walton, and G. Blakemore Evans, eds, *The History of King Henry the Fourth as revised by Sir Edward Dering, Bart* (Charlottesville: University of Virginia Press, 1974).

Williams, William Proctor, "What's a Lost Play?", in *Lost Plays in Shakespeare's England*, ed. David McInnis and Matthew Steggle (Houndsmill: Palgrave Macmillan, 2014), pp. 17–30.

Worthen, W. B., *Shakespeare and the Authority of Performance* (Cambridge: Cambridge University Press, 1997).

Zimmerman, Susan, "The Folger Manuscripts of Thomas Middleton's *A Game at Chesse*: A Study in the Genealogy of Texts," *The Papers of the Bibliographical Society of America*, 76.2 (1982), 159–95.

INDEX

For the benefit of digital users, indexed terms that span two pages (e.g., 52–53) may, on occasion, appear on only one of those pages.

Aeschylus 103–104; *Oresteia* 87
Aldine press 103–104
Ambrosian Palimpsest 6
Anne, Queen 71–72
antimasque 70–71
Ariosto, Ludovico *see* Harington
Aristophanes 68, 103–104; *Knights* 84–85; *Peace* 104
Aristotle, *Poetics* 21, 46–47, 81–82
Ascham, Roger 84–85
audience 1, 8–9, 11, 13–14, 18, 19–21, 23–24, 43–44, 50, 51, 53–54, 64–65, 67–68, 70–72, 75, 76–79, 86–87, 91, 92, 94–95, 98, 100–103, 105–107

Barnes, Barnabe, *The Devil's Charter* 49–50
Barton, Anne 23–24
Bate, Jonathan 92
Beaumont, Francis, *Knight of the Burning Pestle* 9
and John Fletcher, *Comedies and Tragedies* 12, 66, 107
Berger, Harry, Jr. 54–55
black letter type 15, 81
Blackfriars' theater 9, 49–51, 68
Blanchett, Cate 21
Blank, Daniel 86–87
blank verse 1–2, 24–34
Bolsover 78–79
Brook, Peter 64–65, 92
Brooke, Arthur, *Romeus and Juliet* 48
Brower, Reuben 92–94
Bruster, Douglas 23–24
Buckingham, Duke of *see* Villiers

Burbage, Richard 86–87
Butler, Martin 72

Cambises see Preston, Thomas
Cambridge 68, 104
Campion, Thomas, *Lord Hay's Masque* 71–72, 74
Carr, Robert, Earl of Somerset 70
Cary, Elizabeth 14–15
Cavendish, William, Duke of Newcastle 78–79
Chamberlain, John 74–75
Charles I 35–36, 71–72, 77–78, 89–90
Chettle, Henry 1–2
Christ Church College, Oxford 104
Christian IV 72
Cibber, Colley 62
Clare College, Cambridge 87–88
Coleridge, Samuel Taylor 108
Commedia dell'arte 110
Cormack, Bradin 45–46
Craig, Edward Gordon 108–110
Cranach Press *Hamlet* 108–110
Crowne, John, *Thyestes* 98
Cumberbatch, Benedict 105–106

dancing 70–77
Daniel, Samuel 74; *Cleopatra* 64; *Works* 63
Davenant, William, *Macbeth* 10–11, 49, 57–58; *The Tempest* 10, 58, 61–62
Day, John 20
Dee, John 104
Dench, Judi 21
Dennis, John 59–60
Devereux, Robert, 3rd Earl of Essex 65, 70

Dolce, Lodovico 84–85
Donne, John 23–24
Dryden, John 57–58, 87–88; *The Tempest* 10, 61–62; *Troilus and Cressida* 58 and Nathaniel Lee, *Oedipus* 83
Dudley, Robert, Earl of Leicester 18–19
duelling 87
Dutton, Richard 50–51

Eliot, T. S. 88, 92
Elizabeth I 18–21, 71–72, 84–85
Erasmus, Desiderius 84–85
Erne, Lukas 23, 44–46
Essex, Countess of *see* Howard
Essex, Earl of *see* Devereux
Euripides 103–104; *Iphigenia in Aulis* 84–85; *Trojan Women* 84–85
Evans, G. Blakemore 55

Falkland, Lady *see* Cary
Farmer, Alan B. 3, 6–7
folio 3–4
Ford, John, Thomas Dekker, and William Rowley *Witch of Edmonton* 49–50
Forman, Simon 40–44
Freud, Sigmund 81–84

Gager, William, *Ulysses Redux* 104
Gammer Gurton's Needle 81
Garnier, Robert 64
Garrick, David 10–11
Gascoigne, George, and Francis Kinwelmersh *Jocasta* 84–85
gender 53–55
Gildon, Charles 57–58
Globe theater 1
Gorboduc see Norton
Greenblatt, Stephen 36
Greene, Robert 1–2

Harington, John, *Masque of Solomon and Sheba* 72–73; *Orlando Furioso* 55
Harvey, Gabriel 85–87, 108
Hauptmann, Gerhardt 109–110

Heminges, John, and Henry Condell 52
Henry Prince of Wales 71–72, 75
Henry VIII 71–72
Henslowe, Philip 22, 99–100
Herbert, Mary Sidney, Countess of Pembroke 28; *Antonie (Antonius)* 64
Heywood, Jasper, *Thyestes* 95
Heywood, Thomas, *Apology for Actors* 13; *Brazen Age* 13; *Rape of Lucrece* 13–14
Hobson, John 55
Howard, Catherine, Viscountess Cranbourne 75, 77
Howard, Frances, Countess of Essex and Somerset 65, 70, 75, 77
Howard, Thomas, Earl of Suffolk 75
Howell, James 78–79
Hughes, Ted 94
Kempe, William 86–87

Ingleby, C. M., *Shakespere Allusion Book* 42–43
Irving, Henry 62, 108–109

Jack Juggler 85
Jaggard, William 13
James I 50–51, 71–73, 75, 76, 87–88; *Basilicon Doron* 53; *Daemonologie* 53
Johnson, Samuel 59, 108
Jones, Inigo 74, 77–79, 89–90
Jonson, Ben 20–23, 60–61, 100; *Alchemist* 20–21, 49–50, 64–65, 68–70; *Bartholomew Fair* 20–21, 68–69, 77–78; *Catiline* 64–65, 68–69, 77–78; *Chloridia* 77–78 *Cynthia's Revels* 65, 67, 68–69; *Devil is an Ass* 49–50, 70, 77–78; *Epicoene* 65, 68–69; *Every Man in His Humour* 65; *Every Man Out of His Humour* 64, 68–69, 107; *Hymenaei* 65, 70, 74; *Love Restored* 74–75; *Love's Triumph Through Callipolis* 77–78; *Love's*

Welcome at Bolsover 78–79; *Masque of Queens* 49–50; *Neptune's Triumph* 77; *New Inn* 20–21, 77–78; *Ode to Himself* 77–78; *Pleasure Reconciled to Virtue* 76; *Poetaster* 65, 67; *Richard Crookback* 69; *Sejanus* 64–65, 67, 68–69; *Staple of News* 77–78; *Tale of a Tub* 77–78; *Time Vindicated* 77; *Volpone* 20–21, 64–65, 67, 68, 70, 86–87; *Workes* 63

Kemble, John Philip 62
Kermode, Frank 59–61
Kessler, Count Harry 108–109
Kittredge, George Lyman 59
Kyd, Thomas 99–100; *Cornelia* 15, 64; *Soliman and Perseda* 64; *Spanish Tragedy* 22–24, 39, 49–50, 66

Leicester, Earl of *see* Dudley
Leigh, Vivien 92
Lesser, Zachary 3, 6–7, 13–14
Lost Plays Database 6, 10
Lumley, Jane, Lady 84–85

magic 49–51
Manners, Elizabeth Sidney, Countess of Rutland 65
Marlowe, Christopher 2; *Doctor Faustus* 8–9, 15, 49–50, 101–102; *Jew of Malta* 49–50; *Tamburlaine* 8–9, 39, 64, 66
Marston, John 14–15, 23–24; *Malcontent* 49–50; *Wonder of Women* 49–50
masque 70–79, 89–90
Medwall, Henry, *Fulgens and Lucres* 5–6
Menzer, Paul 39, 108
Middleton, Thomas, *The Witch* 49–51
Miller, Arthur 11
Montagu, Walter, *Shepherd's Paradise* 87–88
Mornay, Philippe de 15

Moseley, Humphrey 12, 20–21, 43–44, 66, 107
Mowat, Barbara 6–7

Nashe, Thomas 1–2, 21, 99–100
Newcastle, Duke of *see* Cavendish
Newton, Thomas, *Seneca His Tenne Tragedies* 100
Norton, Thomas, and Thomas Sackville, *Gorboduc* 17, 81, 85

octavo 3–4
Oldcastle, John 49–50
Oedipus complex 83–84
Olivier, Laurence 92, 100
Overbury, Thomas 70; *The Wife* 3–4
Ovid, *Metamorphoses* 86–87, 91, 94
Oxford 68

Padua, University of 55–57
Parnassus plays 86–87
Passionate Pilgrim, The 13
Peacham, Henry 89–90
Peele, George 84–85
Pembroke, Countess of *see* Herbert, Mary Sidney
Plautus 6, 68, 103–104; *Amphitruo* 85; *Menaechmi* 85
Poel, William 36
Pope, Alexander 24–26, 35, 58–61
Popish plot 90–91
Preiss, Richard 9
Preston, Thomas, *Cambises* 15

quarto 3–4

Rainoldes, John 104
Ralph Roister Doister see Udall
Ravenscroft, Edward, *Titus Andronicus* 90–92, 98
revenge drama 87, 91, 98
Riggs, David 23–24
roman type 15, 81, 94
Rowe, Nicholas 105
Ruggle, George, *Ignoramus* 87–88
Rutland, Countess of *see* Manners

Sabol, Andrew 74
St. John's College, Oxford 86–87
Saxo Grammaticus 109–110
Schlegel, Friedrich 109–110
Seneca 81–84, 87–89, 99; *Hercules Furens* 85; *Medea* 88–89; *Oedipus* 81–83, 87; *Thyestes* 87, 89, 91–92, 95
Shakespeare, William 2, 10, 67–68; first folio 65; *All's Well That Ends Well* 67–68; *Antony and Cleopatra* 27; *As You Like It* 1, 52–53, 101; *Comedy of Errors* 52; *Coriolanus* 100; *Hamlet* 4–5, 11, 13–14, 20, 52–53, 68, 86–87, 99–102, 105–106, 108; *Henry IV* 49–50; *1 Henry VI* 21, 52–53, 89, 100; *3 Henry VI* 2, 52–53, 89, 100; *Julius Caesar* 28, 52–53, 60–61; *King Lear* 11–12, 17–18, 75; *Love's Labour's Lost* 67–68, 101; *Macbeth* 10, 40–42, 49, 101–102; *Measure for Measure* 55–56; *Merchant of Venice* 49–50; *Midsummer Night's Dream* 52–53, 86–87; *Othello* 36–37, 100; *Pericles* 11–12; *Rape of Lucrece* 12–13, 86–87; *Richard III* 52–53, 69, 86–87, 89, 100; *Romeo and Juliet* 34, 101, 106–107; *The Tempest* 10, 24–26, 28–29, 36–37, 49–51, 57–59, 61–62, 100; *Titus Andronicus* 89–98; *Troilus and Cressida* 58, 68; *Twelfth Night* 67–68, 101–102, 106–107; *Venus and Adonis* 12–13, 86–87; *Winter's Tale* 35–37, 40, 41–43

Shaw, George Bernard 11
shorthand 13–14
Sir John Oldcastle 49–50
Somerset, Countess of *see* Howard
Somerset, Earl of *see* Carr
Sophocles 6, 103–104; *Oedipus Tyrannos* 81–82, 103–104
Stallybrass, Peter 13–14
Stanislavski, Konstantin 108–109
Stern, Tiffany 13–14, 23–24, 47, 99–100
Suffolk, Earl of *see* Howard

Tate, Nahum, *King Lear* 58
Teatro Olimpico 103–104
Terence 68, 85, 103–104; *Andria* 103–104
Trapolin, G. P., *Antigone* 92
Terry, Ellen 108

Udall, Nicholas, *Ralph Roister Doister* 81, 85

Vickers, Brian 23–24
Villiers, George, Duke of Buckingham 76–77

Walker, Greg, and Henry James 18
Wase, Charles, *Electra* 81–82
Watson, Thomas, *Antigone* 85
Wells, Stanley 60–61
Werstine, Paul 44–45
Williams, William Proctor 10
Williams, Tenessee 11
Wilson, John Dover 35, 109–110
witchcraft 11, 41, 52–55, 101–102, 104, 105
Wittenburg, University of 109

Yeats, William Butler 83–84

The manufacturer's authorised representative in the EU for product
safety is Oxford University Press España S.A. of El Parque Empresarial
San Fernando de Henares, Avenida de Castilla, 2 - 28830 Madrid
(www.oup.es/en or product.safety@oup.com). OUP España S.A. also acts
as importer into Spain of products made by the manufacturer.
Printed and bound by CPI Group (UK) Ltd, Croydon, CR0 4YY

20/03/2026

02075329-0001